CREATIVE GLASS CRAFTS

Painting, Etching,
Stained Glass
& More

CREATIVE GLASS CRAFTS

Marthe Le Van

LARK BOOKS

A Division of Sterling Publishing Co., Inc.
New York

Art Director:
DANA IRWIN

Photographer:
SANDRA STAMBAUGH

Cover Design:
BARBARA ZARETSKY

Assistant Art Director:
HANNES CHAREN

Editorial Assistance:
VERONIKA ALICE GUNTER, RAIN
NEWCOMB, HEATHER SMITH

Proofreader:
KIM CATANZARITE

Library of Congress Cataloging-in-Publication Data

Le Van, Marthe.
   Creative glass crafts : painting, etching, stained glass, and more / by Marthe Le Van.

      p. cm.
   Includes index.
   ISBN 1-57990-430-0
      1. Glass craft–Patterns. I. Title.

TT298 .L429 2002
748–dc21

2001038049

10 9 8 7 6 5 4 3 2 1

Published by Lark Books, a division of
Sterling Publishing Co., Inc.
387 Park Avenue South
New York, N.Y. 10016

First Paperback Edition 2003
© 2002, Lark Books

Distributed in Canada by Sterling Publishing,
c/o Canadian Manda Group, One Atlantic Ave., Suite 105
Toronto, Ontario, Canada M6K 3E7

Distributed in Australia by Capricorn Link (Australia) Pty Ltd.,
P.O. Box 704, Windsor, NSW 2756 Australia

Distributed in the U.K. by Guild of Master Craftsman Publications Ltd.,
Castle Place 166 High Street, Lewes, East Sussex, England, BN7 1XU.
Tel: (+44) 1273 477374 • Fax: (+44) 1273 478606
Email: pubs@thegmcgroup.com • Web: www.gmcpublications.com

If you have questions or comments about this book, please contact:
Lark Books
67 Broadway
Asheville, North Carolina 28801
(828) 253-0467

Printed in China

ISBN 1-57990-430-0

CONTENTS

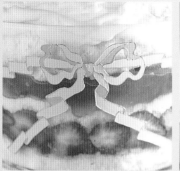   

Introduction

Glass is a captivating material: its sparkling translucence, wondrous reflections, and luminous colors are irresistible. *Creative Glass Crafts* features easy ways to transform glass using paints, etching creams, stained glass techniques, and embellishments. Whether you're enhancing functional glassware such as vases, coasters, and picture frames, or creating decorative pieces such as sun catchers and stained glass panels, you'll be pleased with the professional, attractive effects you can achieve. To make great-looking accessories and home decor accents, all you need is the desire to create and, typically, a single afternoon.

There are many new and remarkable products that expand the possibilities for simple glass crafting. A variety of paints are readily available that bind to the surface of glass. Either air-dried or baked in an oven, these glass paints offer superb opportunities for decorative painting. Glass is an exciting surface to paint. Its natural translucence produces dazzling effects with light. Etching with creams and liquids is another breakthrough. You can frost the surface of glass in a matter of minutes without sandblasting or harsh chemicals. The matte appearance of etched glass always brings a touch of elegance. The thrill of painting and etching glass may inspire you to beautify every glass surface in sight—and why shouldn't you? Since most commercial glass is factory-produced, there's great similarity among vases, plates, and goblets. You like individuality, don't you? Give your glass some personality and it's sure to attract attention.

The stained glass designs in this book are perfect for the beginner. They're small, have a limited number of pieces, use easy-to-find types of glass, and assemble with ease. They're also incredibly stylish. It's no exaggeration to say that you can learn fundamental stained glass skills and create at least one beautiful project in just a weekend.

The last chapter of the book features a variety of unconventional ways to work with glass. It's a lively and diverse collection of simple techniques, including embellishment, decoupage, beading, bottle cutting, and assembly. The projects reflect a variety of styles, too, from luscious florals to Eastern minimalism, and include a wide range of accessories for your home.

Creative Glass Crafts invites you to creatively play with glass. You'll find four basics chapters, each containing a section on materials, tools, and techniques, followed by eight to twelve related projects. Feel free to start with whichever topic interests you the most—painting, etching, stained glass, or embellishment—then sample the other sections. You're sure to find enchanting designs to inspire you and heighten your passion for glass.

Painting on Glass

The arrival of easy, do-it-yourself products means everyone can have fun painting on glass. The variety of glass paints is ever-expanding. From transparent liquids to three-dimensional outliners to sprays that imitate the look of stained glass, there's a product available for every conceivable project. Whether you favor a brush, pen, or tube, high-gloss or matte finish, there's a glass paint to suit your style.

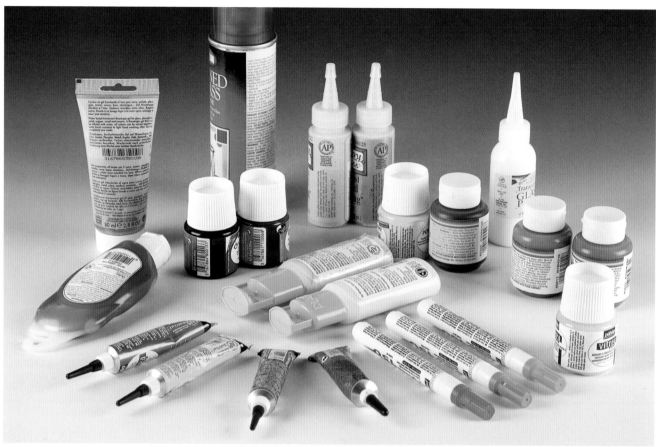

Assorted glass paints

Materials

PAINTS

Each type of paint comes with a printed label of detailed instructions and product information. Before starting any glass painting project, carefully read this text to familiarize yourself with application procedures and drying time.

AIR-DRYING AND THERMOHARDENING PAINTS

Glass paints are either air-drying or thermohardening. Thermohardening paints are baked in a standard household oven after they've completely air-dried. This heat-based curing process is patterned after the more complex process of firing glass enamels. Thermohardening produces a more durable painted surface that withstands increased handling and even washing. Air-drying glass paints are the least durable type and will not withstand washing. Choose to work with these when you are painting a decorative project that won't be handled often. Air-dried paints are great for decorating objects that are too large to fit in a conventional oven.

WATER-BASED AND SOLVENT-BASED PAINTS

Water-based glass paints are easy to use, making them a good choice for beginner glass painters. They're available in a bottle, tube, or spray can, and come in a wide range of transparent, translucent, opaque, and textured tones. Whether you're mixing colors or adding a finish, water-based glass paints are easy to blend. Adding a clear acrylic medium to a water-based paint makes its color more transparent without thinning its consistency. These paints require no measuring or mixing—just stir or shake. They're also a very forgiving medium—any flaws can be quickly wiped away with a moist cotton swab. For added convenience, you can clean paintbrushes used with water-based glass paints with water instead of solvents. These paints are available in both air-drying and thermohardening varieties.

The durability and creative potential of solvent-based glass paints are virtually identical to water-based paints. The majority of colors available in solvent-based paints are transparent with fewer opaque and dimensional options. The chief differences between the paints are procedural. A little extra preparation and a few more materials are required to use solvent-based paints. You'll have to clean your brushes with mineral spirits. Due to the flammability of solvents, it's a good idea to paint in a well-ventilated area. Extra precautions can be taken to increase your safety, such as wearing latex gloves and a mask while working with these products.

RELIEF OUTLINER PAINT

Outliner paint is used to boldly accentuate the edges of a design, or to be the design itself, similar to a line drawing. Outliner paint is the best way to fabricate the look of stained glass lead on a painted project (photo 1). Outliner paint is sold in tubes, primarily in shades of black and metallics. When preparing to use a new outliner tube, snip the tip off as close to the end as possible. This will give you a thin stream of paint and increase your control. Outlining mistakes are easily removed. Let the paint dry thoroughly, and then pick or scrape it off the glass surface with a sharp craft knife.

Photo 1

GEL PAINTS

Gel paints are superb for outlining in three-dimensional color and creating relief effects. They're translucent when dry and have the same durability as other air-dry glass paints. Water-based gel paints are frequently squeezed from a tube, but if shaken or stirred, they'll liquify to a viscosity that permits brush application. Gel paints have a tendency to collect a watery build up. To prevent this residue either give the tube a good shake before use, or drain the liquid onto a paper towel. Gel paints can also be used as colored adhesives in which to embed other objects, such as jewels or beads.

PAINT ALTERNATIVES

Some paints not specifically manufactured for use on glass successfully adapt to this application. You may already have many of these paints around the house but have never thought of using them on glass. Examples of unusual but acceptable glass paints include fabric paints, paint pens, and all-purpose acrylic enamel. Read all compatibility restrictions printed on the paint labels. You may be surprised to see glass listed as a receptive surface. If it isn't, go ahead and test the paint on a glass scrap to determine the results for yourself.

Testing Paints

How transparent or opaque are your new glass paints? Does the paint spread smoothly in a thin layer across the glass, or is it stiff and dimensional? How well-suited is your new paint to different application techniques, such as brushing, stamping, sponging, or piping from a tip? When you buy glass paints, it's a good idea to explore their artistic range on scrap glass before starting your project (photo 2). Your recycling bin is a treasure chest of test-glass surfaces. Empty and clean jam jars and oil bottles are ready and willing subjects for all sorts of

Photo 2

experimentation. Read and observe all the manufacturer's instructions and recommendations prior to working with the paint. Commercial paints are thoroughly tested, and the makers are keenly aware of their individual properties. They provide helpful guidelines to encourage painting success and promote customer satisfaction.

Mixing Paints

An artist's color wheel is a valuable reference tool available at any fine art supply store. It tells you how to mix two or more colors of paint to achieve a new, third color. Using a color wheel can be very cost effective because you gain the knowledge required to mix rather than buy new colors. A color wheel also eliminates the frustration and waste of trial and error blending. When you're color mixing, stick to one brand of paint if possible. Combining different brands may result in incompatibility problems. Not only is it advisable to mix the same brand of paint, it's even better to mix the same product

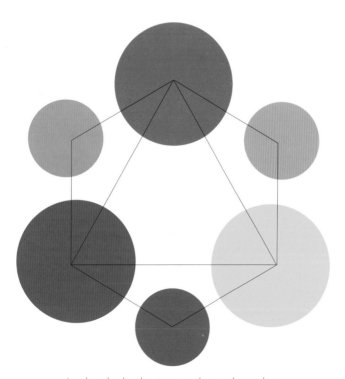

A color wheel with primary and secondary colors

llines within the paint brand. Never mix solvent-based with water-based paints.

GLASS

Glassware is everywhere and the ideas for transforming it are endless. All surfaces are fair game for the budding (and eager) glass painter. Freehand painters are at liberty to decorate any and every

A variety of glass items to decorate

surface to their heart's content. If you're using design templates, flat glass is the ideal practice surface for the beginner.

TOOLS

PALETTE KNIFE

A palette knife is a flat tool used to spoon paint out of its bottle and deposit it onto a mixing palette. It's the best way to stir a single color or to mix two colors together. A palette knife can also spread thick glass paints, such as gels, directly onto glass.

MIXING PALETTE

Mixing palettes are commercially available at art supply stores. They're generally made of plastic, and feature small slots for individual paint colors as well as larger areas for mixing paints. Shallow plastic lids, such as those that top food containers, make perfectly proper palettes. These trays provide easy access to paints and are a practical surface for mixing colors. Use a palette knife to take paint from its jar, designate a palette area for that color, and spread the paint on the tray.

PAINTBRUSHES

A wide variety of brushes will expand the ways you can express yourself with paint. If you're just getting started, a 1-inch (2.5 cm) flat brush, a ¼-inch (6 mm) round brush, and a ⅛-inch (3 mm) fine-tip brush will accommodate your needs. Artist's brushes vary dramatically in quality and price. Buy the best that you can afford, as the lower-quality brushes often shed bristles. This can be a nuisance and cause painting mistakes. Specialty brushes produced for decorative painting are a great addition. In general, they're named for the function they perform—glazing, stippling, stenciling brushes—to name a few. Some paintbrushes aren't brushes at all. Rubber-tip paintbrushes are especially useful to glass painting as they have no bristles. This reduces the likelihood of air bubbles forming while you're painting.

Right: assorted sponges, applicator bottle, applicator tips, combing tool, assorted paintbrushes

CLEANING OLD GLASS

Just because a glass object isn't new doesn't mean it can't be painted. Many older glass items have artistic character not found in contemporary, mass-produced merchandise. Seeking these glass treasures at garage sales and flea markets is a rewarding hobby. Painting historic items, such as milk or tonic bottles, contributes a nostalgic flair. Mix-and-match glass items, such as teacups and plates, frequently have a high relief, molded pattern. The existing decorative motif can be highlighted with paint, accentuating the designs and breathing new life into old glass. Lots of old glass can be bought at a low price, but the pieces will probably need some cleaning. Years of dirt and grime may have made them a little drab. One easy cleaning solution is to soak the dull glass in a mixture of one cup (.24 L) ammonia and four cups (.96 L) water for a few hours or, preferably, overnight. This technique lifts off build-up and revitalizes the glass to a near-original sheen. If there's residual sediment trapped at the bottom of a glass and the deposit is impossible to clean by hand, fill the object with white vinegar and allow it to stand for a few days. Unwanted dirt particles will disappear when you pour the vinegar out.

APPLICATOR BOTTLES AND TIPS

An optional way to apply glass paint is by using a plastic applicator bottle. Squeezing paint through the tip of an upturned bottle is a process similar to cake decorating. Different plastic or metal applicator tips alter the look of your line. Depending upon the tip, the lines can vary greatly in width and depth. Some applicator tips even produce three-part lines for whimsical stars and squiggles. Remember to read the label to determine if the paint will work with specific tips.

SPONGES

Sponges press paint onto the glass surface rather than brush it on. They bring a fun, fresh element to glass painting. Kitchen sponges, cosmetic sponges, sea sponges, and pre-cut commercial sponges can all be put to use with great effect. They can be cut into any shape (photo 3). Rough sponges apply paint in fascinating, asymmetrical ways that build texture.

Photo 3

COMBING OR REDUCTIVE TOOLS

You can drag many simple tools through wet paint to achieve decorative patterns (photo 4). The design you create comes from negative space where no paint is on the glass. This is called *reductive painting*. Using a comb is the reductive method most

Photo 4

widely practiced, although toothpicks, knitting needles, and erasers also render spectacular results. For an example of the reductive technique, see A Table To Dine For on page 26.

CUTTING TOOLS

A sharp craft knife with changeable blades is a beneficial tool for crafters in any field. A stationery, or fixed, blade allows you to cut out accurate lines down the length of a straightedge, while blades that pivot 360° help with curves and intricate patterns. Both of these blades cut self-adhesive vinyl (especially useful for making stencils) and simulated lead lines. A heavy-duty retractable craft knife makes large cuts where precision isn't required. Scissors are also indispensable. If possible, have a large-bladed and small-bladed pair on hand to tackle any project from cutting sponges to delicate template work.

MEASURING TOOLS

Rulers made of metal are qualified to perform many tasks. They can function as an accurate measuring devise, a straightedge for marking lines, and a sturdy cutting guide for your craft knife.

TAPE

Masking tape and transparent tape are essential materials for fastening a template under or behind glass for tracing or holding papers in place for a carbon paper transfer. Painter's tape, masking tape, or duct tape can also be used as a painting resist. Strips of tape can mask straight lines on the surface of the glass and even form striped and geometric patterns. Make sure to flatten the edges of the tape to prevent the paint from seeping underneath your mask.

MISCELLANEOUS TOOLS AND MATERIALS

Ordinary tweezers are ideal for gripping small objects and embedding them into glass paint. Toothpicks and straight pins are used to smooth paint, pop air bubbles, and make marks. Cotton-tipped swabs and cotton balls aid in preparing

Miscellaneous tools and materials

glass surfaces and eliminating painting mistakes. Another useful item is a pick-out tool. It resembles a craft knife but with only the top part of the sharp blade. This tool can remove the cut-away part of a stencil from its center point without disturbing the surrounding vinyl.

Techniques
THE PROCESS

A simple, standardized series of three basic steps applies to all methods of glass painting.

1. Clean and prepare the surface of the glass. Remove all stickers, price tags, and labels. Wash the glass in warm, soapy water to remove dirt, oils, and other residue. Rinse the glass with warm water and dry it thoroughly. Wipe the surface of the glass with a cotton ball moistened with isopropyl alcohol. The alcohol acts as a surface conditioner for the glass.

2. Paint the glass.

3. Seal your design.

All applied glass paint needs to dry thoroughly to secure the design. To achieve the proper seal, always follow the recommendations printed on your paint bottle. This process may be as simple as air-drying the glass object over a matter of days. Other paints may require oven baking to bond them onto the glass and achieve their most durable state. Once the glass paints are cured, you can add a glaze or gloss top coat to give a polished appearance. These finishing products come in a several finishes, such as matte, satin, semi-gloss, high gloss, or crackle.

TRANSFERRING PATTERNS

If you choose to copy a pattern rather than to paint freehand, it becomes necessary to secure the design in place. There are three tried-and-true ways to transfer a design template prior to painting. The first is to use tape to stick the pattern to the back side of the glass (photo 5). If you're painting a vessel and can't use tape, fill the space behind the pattern with round beans or grains (photo 6). The transparency of glass lets you follow the pattern lines accurately as you outline or paint. This method doesn't work on mirrored glass. The second method is to cut closely

Photo 5

Photo 6

around your design, tape or hold it tightly to your glass, and trace its contour with a water-based permanent marker or a china marker. Use this tracing as your painting guide. The third method is the carbon paper transfer. Position the carbon side of the paper to face the glass and lay it on the surface. Place your drawing on top of the carbon paper and use tape or rubber bands to fasten both sheets firmly in place. Follow the lines of your drawing with a ballpoint pen to complete the transfer (photo 7).

Photo 8

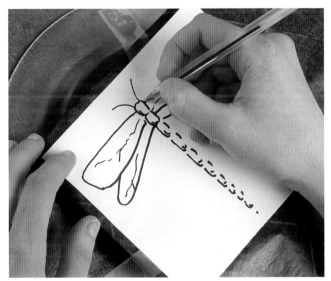

Photo 7

Photo 9

OUTLINING

You can enhance the appeal of your glass paintings with dramatic outlines and borders. A special type of glass paint, called relief outliner or contour paint, is available in a variety of colors and thicknesses. It simulates the look of lead for a painted stained glass project or delineates color fields for other compositions. Outliners are often sold in bottles or tubes that have a narrow applicator tip. The tip allows you to draw your lines with ease. Practice improves your outlining skills, so keep several scrap glass surfaces handy. They'll be useful as you familiarize yourself with the feel of different outliners as you pre-

pare to paint. To create a clean solid line, touch the outliner tip to the surface of the glass. When you're confident that you've made solid contact, lift the tip just above your painting surface while applying consistent pressure, and move the tube along the direction of your drawing (photo 8). Press the outliner tip back down on the glass only when you're ready to complete a line. Pressing the tip to the glass in the middle of a line will stop the flow of outliner and create a gap in the paint. An alternative way to paint with outliners is to touch the tip to the glass and drag it along with steady pressure (photo 9). This method produces a more casual line quality. Under-outlining is an interesting reverse glass painting technique. It's practical to use on projects with flat glass surfaces such as the Early Bird Tray on page 40. Another technique is to embed decorative objects directly into thick outliner paint. Beads and small glass jewels require no fixative when they're applied this way.

MASKING

When you mask a surface, you're blocking off areas you don't want to expose to paint. Masking tape is a convenient way to lay out precise linear patterns. Easy tape-masking options include parallel stripes and geometric grids. Another masking technique for glass painting uses spray fixative. Any interesting pattern can be a paint resist if it's not too fragile or cherished. Found objects such as doilies and leaves work well. You can also cut out shapes from paper or vellum. Once you select your resist, spray the back side with adhesive, place the resist on the glass, smooth it down, and allow the fixative to dry completely. Then, paint around, and even over, the resist to complete your project. Allow your paint to dry for the length of time recommended by the manufacturer. Leave the resist in place during this time (as long as a couple of days). Once the drying time is complete, remove the resist. A pick-out tool helps detach the resist without disturbing the paint.

STENCILING

Stenciling is painting through a hole or a pattern of holes that form a design. A stencil is made of a material that can be adhered to glass. Stencils are either purchased pre-cut from a store or homemade. The simplest stencil can be produced from heavyweight paper such as poster board. This stencil

material is satisfactory only for a single use. If you make your stencil from a water-repellant substance, such as acetate, it can be recycled any number of times. Stenciling is an excellent way to replicate the same motif all over a glass surface.

SPONGING

Sponging paint onto glass creates many surface effects. Applying the paint sparingly with a textured sponge gives a soft and luminous appearance. With greater manual pressure, a sponge's surface makes more contact with the glass. This results in thicker, more uniform paint coverage. Using a little more pressure in consecutive spongings yields a graduated intensity of tone across the surface area of the glass. An interesting multi-color blending occurs when you sponge with more than one color in an area. To sponge, pour the glass paint onto a mixing palette, plastic lid, or plastic plate. Hold the sponge level and press it into the paint. Check that the sponge is lightly and evenly covered with paint

Photo 10

on a test-surface before pressing it onto the glass. Design elements with simple contours such as stars, dots, and diamonds can be cut out of both textured and flat sponges. Repeating these shapes along an edge or over the entire surface of the glass forms interesting patterns and borders (photo 10). The technique of sponging is suitable for any material that will hold paint. A wadded-up piece of newspaper, a crumpled plastic bag, or a bunch of nubby fabric all create spectacular paint effects.

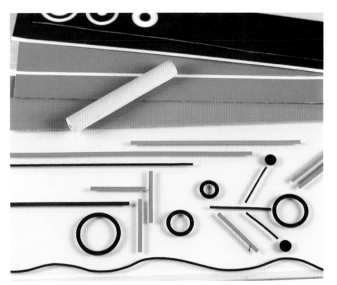

Self-adhesive simulated lead with a small dowel for burnishing

STAMPING

Store-bought stamps are widely available in a myriad of designs from letters to lions to lighthouses. If one strikes your fancy, try it on glass with paint or permanent ink. You can also make your own original stamps out of fruits, vegetables, or rubber erasures. Draw a design, carve it out, and get stamping. Patterned found objects make great stamps in their unaltered state. Use the natural beauty of leaves, feathers, and mushroom caps to make an earthy statement, or stamp on paint with lace or doilies for a delicate texture.

SELF-ADHESIVE SIMULATED LEAD

This self-adhesive plastic product comes in many shapes, widths, and colors. Multiple concentric circles or straight strips of plastic are sold attached to a backing paper. Peel away and discard the paper before pressing the simulated lead onto the glass surface and securing it in place (photo 11). It's easy to cut the stripping to any length, bend it into any shape, and fill the interior with paint (photo 12) to create beautiful and unique designs such as the Golden Moment Panel on page 33, Galaxy Lamp on page 36, and A Dashing Frame on page 38.

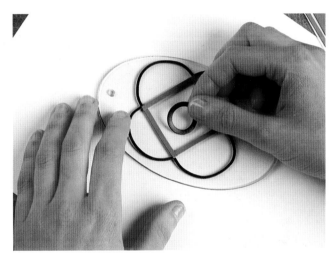

Photo 11

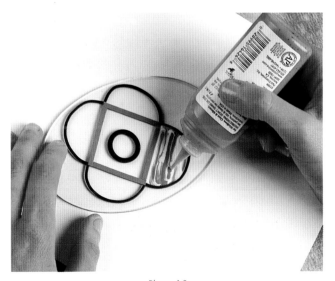

Photo 12

Charming, Swarming Vases

Designer
DIANA LIGHT

PERFECT FOR DAISIES AND DAFFODILS, THESE CHEERFUL MINI-VASES ARE AS FRESH AS SPRING BLOSSOMS. FINE-TIP PAINT PENS OFFER THE CONTROL YOU NEED TO PRODUCE DELICATE INSECT WINGS AND TINY ANTENNAE. CREATE A SWARM ON EACH VASE BY REPEATING THE MOTIF, AND CATCH THE GLASS PAINTING BUG!

What You Need

4 glass bud vases

Water-based, thermohardening transparent glass paint pens in light blue, dark blue, orange, and brown

Glass cleaner

Paper towels, or a lint-free cloth

Photocopy of design templates sized to fit your vases (page 155)

Transparent tape, or round beans or grains

Scrap flat glass or paper

Cotton-tipped swabs

Scissors

Oven

What You Do

1 Remove all labels and adhesive from the glass. Clean the vases with glass cleaner and a paper towel or lint-free cloth.

2 Trim the photocopied patterns to fit inside the vases. Secure each pattern on the interior surface of the glass with transparent tape, or by filling the vases with round beans or grains.

3 Start the paint flow from the pens according to the manufacturer's instructions. Test the paint pens on the scrap flat glass or paper until they produce an even and satisfactory flow.

4 Choose one outline-color pen, and paint the appropriate contour area of the bugs. Let the outline paint dry completely before switching colors. Select a second outline-color pen, and finish painting the bugs' contour. Let the second color dry.

5 Select one interior-color paint pen and fill in the spaces you outlined in step 4. Once all the spaces painted with the first interior-color pen are dry, begin painting with the second interior-color pen. You now have fully painted bugs. Allow them to dry. If any color appears too light, gently paint a second coat directly on top of the first.

6 Paint pens are perfect for decorating your new bug vases with tiny, fanciful dots. Paint borders of dots around the rim of the bee and ladybug vases. Add a gentle curve of dots underneath the butterfly and the dragonfly to suggest their flight patterns.

7 Remove any paint flaws with a moist cotton-tipped swab. Let the painted vases dry. Bake the vases in your oven following the instructions printed on the paint pen packaging.

Provincial Panes

GIVE NEW LIFE TO A HUMDRUM PIECE OF FURNITURE OR ENRICH THE SIMPLE GLASS DOORS ON YOUR KITCHEN CABINETS WITH THIS STYLIZED MOTIF. A SINGLE COLOR OF OUTLINER PAINT TURNS PLAIN GLASS PANES INTO A DECORATOR'S DREAM.

What You Do

1 Clean the exterior surface of the glass panes with glass cleaner and a paper towel or lint-free cloth.

2 Arrange the photocopied design templates on the glass panes of your cabinet. In the photograph, note that the designer fully covered the glass panes by repeating the pattern two or four times. To accomplish this, use one pattern's bottom row of dots as the top row of the pattern underneath. You may choose to center only one pattern on a pane, or adapt the design in other ways to suit the glass. When you're satisfied with the arrangement, make note of the pattern placement.

3 Attach a design template to the interior surface of a glass pane with transparent tape. Make sure the pattern is level. On scrap flat glass or paper, test the line quality of the tube of outliner paint. Become familiar with the amount of manual pressure needed to achieve and maintain satisfactory paint flow.

4 Following the design template, make small dots on the outside surface of the glass. To avoid smearing the dots as you paint, begin at the top of the design and work towards the bottom. Let the outliner paint dry. If you aren't pleased with the appearance of a dot or a series of dots, wait for the paint to dry, then scrape it off with the tip of a craft knife blade.

5 Repeat steps 3 and 4 for each pane of glass.

What You Need

*Cabinet with glass-pane doors

Water-based, air-drying relief outliner paint in white or pearl

Glass cleaner

Paper towels, or a lint-free cloth

Photocopies of design template sized to fit your panes (below)

Transparent tape

Fixed-blade craft knife

Scrap flat glass or paper

Cotton-tipped swabs

If desired, paint the exterior of the cabinet blue and the interior a rich orange. Painting the interior of your cabinet contrasts the painted designs on the glass door.

Fanciful Trifle Tureen

Designer
DIANA LIGHT

PRESENT LAYER UPON LAYER OF DELECTABLE GOODIES WITH STYLE IN THIS PRETTY TRIFLE BOWL. CREATING THE FLOWING RIBBON AND BOW MOTIF HELPS BUILD YOUR OUTLINING SKILLS. YOUR HOLIDAY DESSERT OR POT-LUCK SALAD WILL TASTE EVEN BETTER SERVED IN THIS FESTIVE DISH.

What You Do

1 Clean the exterior surface of the glass with glass cleaner and a paper towel or lint-free cloth. Determine the front of the bowl. Use pieces of transparent tape to adhere the photocopied bow pattern to the interior surface of the bowl at its front center point.

2 On the scrap flat glass or paper, practice outlining with the tube of gold paint. For a description of different outlining techniques, refer to page 15. Whenever you're satisfied with the quality of the outliner, begin applying the gold lines of paint on top of the bow pattern. After painting all the lines, let the gold outliner dry. Scrape off any outlining mistakes with the tip of the craft knife blade as soon as the paint is dry.

3 Arrange the ribbon pattern on the interior surface of the bowl so that its design flows uninterrupted from the bow. The design can start on either side of the bow. Affix the ribbon pattern in place with pieces of transparent tape.

4 Apply the outlines of gold paint on top of the ribbon pattern. After painting all the lines, let the gold outliner dry.

5 Reposition the ribbon pattern on the interior surface of the bowl so that it flows uninterrupted from the segment of ribbon painted in step 4.

6 Repeat steps 4 and 5 approximately six times, or until you create enough ribbon segments to circle the bowl and reconnect with the bow.

7 Mix the light peach glass paint according to the manufacturer's instructions. Pour a little of the paint into a plastic applicator bottle. Select a small applicator tip, attach it to the top of the bottle,

What You Need

Glass trifle bowl, approximately 8¾ x 8½ inches (21.9 x 20.3 cm)

Water-based, air-drying relief outliner in gold

Water-based, air-drying glass paint in light peach and dark peach

Glass cleaner

Paper towels, or a lint-free cloth

Photocopy of design templates sized to fit your bowl (page 154)

Plastic applicator bottle

Small applicator bottle tip

Transparent tape

Scrap flat glass or paper

Cotton-tipped swabs

and make a secure connection. Practice painting with the applicator bottle on scrap flat glass or paper. Fill in all the outlined highlight areas with the light peach paint. Remove any paint from on top of the gold outliner with a moist cotton-tipped swab.

8 Mix the dark peach glass paint. Pour a little of the paint into a clean plastic applicator bottle and attach a small tip. Fill in all remaining outlined areas with the dark peach paint. These sections are the shadows. Remove any paint from on top of the gold outliner with a moist cotton-tipped swab. Allow the paints to dry for the amount of time recommended by the manufacturer.

Meditation Mirror

A QUIET REFLECTION OF NATURE, THIS MIRROR'S PRESENCE ADDS SERENITY TO ANY ROOM. WISPY BRANCHES OF BITTERSWEET OUTLINED WITH GLASS PAINTS SUGGEST THE LOOK OF GENUINE LEAD.

What You Need

Round mirror, 12 inches (30.5 cm) in diameter

Water-based, air-drying simulated stained glass paints in brown, amber, and red-orange

Water-based, air-drying simulated lead paint in black

Glass cleaner

Paper towels, or a lint-free cloth

Photocopy of design template sized to fit your mirror (page 155)

Carbon paper

Transparent tape

Plastic applicator bottle

Small applicator tip

Scrap flat glass or paper

Cotton-tipped swabs

Straight pin

Ballpoint pen or pencil

Craft knife

What You Do

1 Clean the mirror with the glass cleaner and a paper towel or lint-free cloth.

2 Use carbon paper to transfer the design template onto the surface of the mirror. Directions for making a carbon paper transfer are on page 14.

3 Prepare the simulated lead paint according to manufacturer's instructions. Pour the paint into the plastic applicator bottle, place the small applicator tip into the top of the bottle, and make a tight seal. On the scrap flat glass or paper, practice painting with the applicator bottle and the simulated lead paint until you're satisfied with the results.

4 Carefully paint along all the lines of the transferred design. Allow the paint to dry.

5 Prepare the simulated stained glass paints. Pour one color of paint into the plastic applicator bottle and attach a clean small applicator tip. Fill in the outlined areas with the first color you've selected to use.

6 Repeat step 5 with the two other colors of simulated stained glass paint. Allow the paints to dry. Eliminate any mistakes by using the tip of the craft knife blade to gently scrape unwanted paint off the surface of the mirror.

25

PAINTING ON GLASS

A Table to Dine For

Designer
DIANA LIGHT

THE ESSENCE OF TASTEFUL LIVING IS REFLECTED IN THE GORGEOUS MAHOGANY PAINT, CONTEMPORARY SPIRALS, AND SUBTLE CRACKLE FINISH OF THIS GLASS-TOP DINING TABLE. PAINTED IN REVERSE, THE TABLETOP WILL SERVICE YOUR CASUAL DINNERS OR SOPHISTICATED GATHERINGS FOR YEARS TO COME.

What You Need

Glass tabletop, 36 inches (.9 m) in diameter

5 bottles water-based, air-drying transparent glass paint in mahogany

1 bottle diluter for water-based, air-drying transparent glass paint

1 bottle crackle medium for water-based, air-drying glass paint

Glass cleaner

Paper towels, or a lint-free cloth

Flat paintbrush, 1 inch (2.5 cm) wide

Rubber combing tool, or pencil eraser

Sturdy cardboard, 36 x 36 inches (.9 x .9 m)

Fixed-blade craft knife

Latex gloves

Marking pen

Newspaper

Scrap flat glass

Cotton-tipped swabs

Straight pin

Clear plastic self-adhesive rubber picture frame bumpers

What You Do

1 Prepare the brown air-drying glass paint. With the flat 1-inch-wide (2.5 cm) brush, paint a small test area on the scrap glass. Monitor the drying time of the paint to determine when it becomes most receptive to combing. For a description of combing and other reductive painting techniques, see page 13.

2 Spread a generous amount of newspaper on a work surface large enough to accommodate the glass tabletop, and lay the glass flat on top. Remember that in this reverse painting project the color is applied to the underside of the glass.

3 Wearing a pair of latex gloves, pour a liberal amount of the glass paint onto the center of the tabletop. Working in a spiral motion that grows larger and larger, quickly spread the paint toward the edges of the glass with your hands. Use a straight pin to pop any bubbles that appear in the paint.

4 Let the paint dry on the glass for the amount of time determined in step 1. Use a rubber combing tool or a pencil eraser to wipe off a spiral of paint that's approximately 2 inches (5 cm) away from the edge of the glass. Clean the paint off the combing tool or pencil eraser with a paper towel before making the next spiral. Continue making spirals around the edge of the tabletop. Adjoining spirals should rotate in different directions. Because you're using a reductive freehand style of painting, expect slight differences in the shape and size of the spirals.

5 Let the glass paint dry for the amount of time recommended by the manufacturer. Clean off

any excess paint left inside the clear spirals with a moist cotton-tipped swab.

6 Use the marking pen to draw a circle with a 24-inch (60 cm) diameter in the center of the cardboard. Beginning in the middle of the circle, use the craft knife to cut the circle out of the cardboard. The original piece of cardboard, with a circle cut out of its center, is the template. Center the hole over the tabletop surface and lay the template down. Hold the cardboard down by placing a heavy object such as a book or a rock on each of the four corners.

7 Prepare the crackle medium. Have a clean, flat paintbrush at the ready. Pour a generous amount of medium in the center of the exposed painted glass surface. Start at the circle's edge and quickly work the crackle medium toward the center of the tabletop. Use big, concentric brush strokes to cover the entire surface. Allow the medium to dry.

8 Adhere the clear rubber picture frame bumpers to the table base to protect the painted glass surface.

Flowering Sun Catchers

Designer
DIANA LIGHT

These lovely floral sun catchers offer year-round delight. Splendid designs, a fine gold outline, and brilliant colors combine with a painterly application to create champion blooms.

What You Need

2 round glass sun catchers, 5 inches (12.7 cm) in diameter

2 oval glass sun catchers, 3¼ x 5 inches (8.1 cm x 12.7 cm)

1 oval glass sun catcher, 2¾ x 4 inches (6.9 x 10.2 cm)

*Water-based, air-drying transparent glass paints in lemon yellow, deep blue, emerald green, orange, scarlet, light violet, and dark violet

*Water-based, air-drying relief outliner in gold

Glass cleaner

Paper towels, or a lint-free cloth

Photocopies of design templates sized to fit your sun catchers (page 32)

Fine-tip artist's paintbrush

Transparent tape

Rinse cup of water

Cotton-tipped swabs

Scrap flat glass or paper

Gloss varnish, optional

Matte varnish, optional

*Oven-baked paints may be substituted in this project.

What You Do

1 Clean both sides of one blank sun catcher with glass cleaner and a paper towel or lint-free cloth.

2 Roll two small pieces of the transparent tape into double-sided sticky tubes. Place one tape tube near the top of the pattern and one tape tube near the bottom of the pattern. Position the sun catcher over the pattern and press it down. The tape tubes hold the pattern in place.

3 Practice painting with the tube outliner on the scrap flat glass or paper. Get a feel for the density of the paint and the speed and pressure at which it flows. Different outlining techniques are explained on page 15. Use whichever outlining technique is most comfortable for you and produces the best result.

4 Follow the lines of the pattern as you paint the gold outliner onto the glass. Let the outliner paint dry.

5 Mix one transparent glass paint. Painting with a fine-tip artist's brush helps you control the glass paint and work it into narrow outlined areas with added precision. Dip the brush into the paint, and apply it in the center of a designated color area on the glass. Push the paint up to the gold outliner borders without painting over them. Continue to work in one color until all designated areas are covered. Clean your paintbrush with water.

Tips

To obtain a lighter shade of a color without changing its transparency, mix the paint with gloss varnish. To give the color a frosted appearance that is less transparent when it's dry, mix the paint with matte varnish.

Use light-fast colors for all painted glass crafts that will receive extended exposure to direct sunlight.

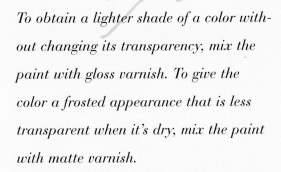

6 Repeat step 5 using a second color of transparent glass paint. Continue with this process until every color has been used and the sun catcher is fully painted. Let the paint dry.

7 Repeat steps 1 through 6 for each sun catcher.

Golden Moment Panel

Designer

DIANA LIGHT

CURRENTS OF COLOR SWIRL AROUND SMOOTH PEBBLE SHAPES ON THIS VIBRANT GLASS PANEL. SIMULATED LEAD STRIPS ACT AS THICK BORDERS TO DEFINE BOTH CURVED ORGANIC CONTOURS AND STRAIGHT FORMAL EDGING. THIS PANEL PROVIDES AN EXCELLENT OPPORTUNITY FOR EXPLORING GLASS PAINTING TECHNIQUES.

What You Need

Flat glass panel, 8½ x 11 inches (21.6 x 27.9 cm)

Self-adhesive simulated lead lines, ⅛-inch-wide (3 mm), in lead-gray

Self-adhesive simulated lead lines, 1/16-inch-wide (2 mm), in lead-gray

Water-based, air-drying simulated lead paint, in lead-gray

Water-based, air-drying simulated stained glass paints in amber, yellow, ivory, royal blue, light blue, red, and brown

Glass cleaner

Paper towels, or a lint-free cloth

Photocopy of design template sized to fit your glass (page 35)

Transparent tape

Fixed-blade craft knife

Plastic applicator bottle

Applicator tips

Cotton-tipped swabs

Scrap flat glass or paper

Straight pin

Toothpicks (optional)

What You Do

1 Clean both sides of the flat glass panel with glass cleaner and a paper towel or lint-free cloth.

2 Place the photocopied template on your work surface and lay the glass panel on top, making sure to center the design beneath the glass. Attach the design template to the glass panel with pieces of transparent tape.

3 With the fixed-blade craft knife, cut lengths of the ⅛-inch-wide (3 mm) simulated lead line to fit the border design. Peel the backing paper away from the simulated lead line and discard. Apply the lead line to the glass, working from the outside of the design in, following the template. Where two or more lines intersect, do not overlap the simulated lead line. Instead, carefully cut the lines to join where they meet.

4 With the fixed-blade craft knife, cut lengths of the 1/16-inch-wide (2 mm) simulated lead lines to make the interior design borders. Peel the backing paper away and discard. Apply the lead line to the glass, carefully cutting the lines to join where they meet.

5 Prepare the simulated-lead glass paint. Pour a small amount of the paint into the plastic applicator bottle. Place the small applicator tip into the top of the bottle and form a tight seal. Practice painting with the applicator bottle on the scrap flat glass or paper. Lightly apply the simulated-lead paint over every place where the lead lines meet. Let the paint dry. This step gives the panel a more authentic stained glass look.

6 Prepare the simulated stained glass paints. Pour a small amount of one of the paints into the clean plastic applicator bottle and attach a small applicator tip. Practice painting with the applicator bottle on the scrap flat glass or paper. When using the stained glass paints, work from the center of the design outward to avoid touching the wet paint. Fill in as many pebbles and flower petals as you wish with the first color. Remember to clean out the applicator bottle and the tip before painting with a new color.

7 Fill in all areas on the panel with the glass paint. Pop any air bubbles that appear in the paint with the straight pin. To swirl paints, apply a thin coat of the main color, then squeeze a little of a secondary color on top of the first in a spiral motion. Use the applicator tip or toothpick to swirl (but not blend) the paints. When swirling, extend the second color all the way to, or even over, the lead line. Then wipe off any excess paint with a moist cotton-tipped swab. This creates the illusion of the color running all the way through, rather than sitting on top of, the glass. As you paint, vary the swirling techniques in areas with distinct colors. Drag the applicator tip or toothpick through the paint in an angular or zigzag fashion to produce simulated stained glass of a different style. Before handling the finished panel, allow the paint to dry.

Galaxy Lamp

Designer
DIANA LIGHT

DOZENS OF DAZZLING ORBS TRANSFORM THIS ORDINARY LAMP INTO A FOCAL POINT FOR ANY CONTEMPORARY SETTING. IT FEATURES SELF-ADHESIVE SIMULATED LEAD CIRCLES AND GLISTENING METALLIC GLASS PAINTS IN A SIMPLE YET IMPRESSIVE DESIGN.

What You Need

Lamp with glass base

Self-adhesive simulated lead circles in gold and silver

Water-based, air-drying simulated lead glass paints in gold and silver

Glass cleaner

Paper towels, or a lint-free cloth

Plastic applicator bottle

Small applicator tips

Cotton-tipped swabs

Straight pin

Scrap flat glass or paper

What You Do

1 Clean the lamp base with glass cleaner and a paper towel or lint-free cloth.

2 Peel the backing paper off one self-adhesive simulated lead circle (either color) and press the circle on the surface of the lamp base. Repeat this step in a random fashion until you're content with the number of applied circles. Alternate between gold and silver circles. In a few areas, place smaller circles inside of larger circles. After pressing the circles firmly in place, clean off any excess adhesive with a moist cotton-tipped swab.

3 Mix the simulated lead glass paint, and pour a little paint into a clean plastic applicator bottle. Select an applicator tip, attach it to the top of the bottle, and make a tight seal. Practice painting with the applicator bottle on scrap flat glass or paper until you feel comfortable with the flow of the paint.

4 Use the applicator bottle to paint inside the self-adhesive lead circles. Use a straight pin to pop any bubbles that appear in the paint. Remove any paint from on top of the simulated lead circles with a moist cotton-tipped swab. Allow the paint to dry.

5 Repeat steps 3 and 4 with the second color of glass paint. Keep in mind that silver and gold look great next to each other or used individually.

A Dashing Frame

Designer
DIANA LIGHT

BOLD BORDERS AND ANGLE
ACCENTS GIVE THIS SLEEK
FRAME ARCHITECTURAL
APPEAL. SIMULATED LEAD
LINES AND A SINGLE COLOR
OF PAINT ARE ALL IT TAKES
TO COMPLETE THIS DAPPER
FRAME.

What You Do

1 Clean both sides of the picture frame glass with glass cleaner and a paper towel or lint-free cloth.

2 Place the photocopied template on your work surface with the design facing up. Place the glass on top of the template, and make sure that the design is centered and level. Using pieces of transparent tape, secure the template to the glass.

3 Peel one self-adhesive lead line off the backing paper. Press the lead line onto the glass following the design template. Use the fixed-blade craft knife to cut the lead line to the necessary length. Where two or more lines intersect, do not overlap the simulated lead lines. Instead, carefully cut the lines to join where they meet. Continue to apply the lead lines until the design is complete.

4 Mix the green simulated stained glass paint. Pour a small amount of the paint into the plastic applicator bottle. Attach the small applicator tip to the top of the bottle and make a tight seal. Fill in the small squares and triangles with the green stained glass paint. Use a straight pin to pop any air bubbles that appear in the paint. Allow the paint to dry.

What You Need

Glass clip frame, 5 x 7 inches (12.7 x 17.8 cm)

Self-adhesive simulated lead lines, 1/8-inch-wide (3 mm), in silver

Water-based, air-drying simulated stained glass paint in green

Glass cleaner

Paper towels, or a lint-free cloth

Photocopy of design template (below) sized to fit your glass

Transparent tape

Fixed-blade craft knife

Plastic applicator bottle

Small applicator tip

Cotton-tipped swabs

Straight pin

Early Bird Tray

Designer
DIANA LIGHT

THIS ELEGANT TRAY IS PERFECT FOR ALL YOUR MEMORABLE MORNING BREAKFASTS AND AFTERNOON TEAS. YOU'LL ENJOY TRANSFORMING A PLAIN GLASS SURFACE INTO A WORK OF ART BASED ON THE RICH TRADITION OF REVERSE GLASS PAINTING.

What You Do

1 Place the photocopied design template on your work surface with the design side facing up. Clean both sides of the glass with glass cleaner and a paper towel or lint-free cloth. Lay the glass over the pattern. Use pieces of transparent tape to attach the pattern to the glass.

2 On the scrap flat glass or paper, practice painting with the tube of copper outliner. For a description of different outlining techniques, refer to page 15. When you're comfortable with the paint flow from the outliner, begin working on the glass. Follow the pattern lines with the copper outliner. Take special care that the outliner makes contact with the glass, especially where two or more lines meet. When the design is complete, let the outliner dry. Scrape any outlining mistakes off the glass surface with a craft knife.

3 Prepare the violet paint. Pour a small amount of paint directly onto the outlined surface of the glass. Spread the paint with the 1-inch-wide (2.5 cm) flat brush. Make horizontal brush stokes across the glass. Add more paint to the glass surface as needed until all areas are covered. Heighten the interest of the violet background by alternating bands of thinly and thickly applied paint.

4 Allow the painted glass to dry. Turn over the glass and place it into the tray with the painted side down.

What You Need

Tray with clear glass inset

*Water-based, air-drying relief outliner in copper

*Water-based, air-drying transparent paint in violet

Glass cleaner

Paper towels, or a lint-free cloth

Photocopy of design template (below) sized to fit the glass in your tray

Flat paintbrush, 1 inch (2.5 cm) wide

Transparent tape

Fixed-blade craft knife

Cotton-tipped swabs

Scrap flat glass or paper

*Oven-baked paints may be substituted in this project.

Time Zone

Designer
DIANA LIGHT

THE UNIQUE AND
DYNAMIC QUALITIES OF
TRANSPARENT GLASS
SPRAY PAINTS PARADE
ACROSS THE FACE OF
THIS CLOCK. THREE BOLD
HUES GRADUALLY BLEND
TO CREATE A SPECTRUM
OF COLOR. GRAPHIC
STENCILS NOT ONLY
PROVIDE EASY-TO-READ
NUMBERS BUT CAST
TERRIFIC SHADOWS
THROUGHOUT THE
COURSE OF THE DAY.

What You Do

1 With the purchased clock movement in hand, visit your local glass supplier. Have a custom circle cut, 9 inches (22.9 cm) in diameter. Base the thickness of the glass on the depth of the clock movement's post. Have a hole drilled in the exact center of the glass circle. The diameter of the hole must accommodate the width of the clock movement's post. For safety in handling, ask the glazier to polish the edges of the glass circle.

2 Lay the white self-adhesive vinyl on a clean work surface and place the glass circle on top. With the pen or pencil, draw a line on the vinyl around the glass circle. Make the line ¼ to ½ inch (6 mm to 1.3 cm) wider than the diameter of the glass. Remove the glass, and cut out the vinyl circle with scissors.

3 Clean the glass with the glass cleaner and a paper towel or lint-free cloth. Place the glass on your work surface. Peel away a small section of the backing paper from the self-adhesive vinyl circle. Allow the edge of the vinyl to extend past the edge of the glass circle by ¼ to ½ inch (6 mm to 1.3 cm). Lightly press down the vinyl once you reach the glass. Peel away more backing paper, and press down more vinyl a little at a time. Use a squeegee to smooth out any air bubbles as you move across the glass. Once the vinyl is completely attached to the glass, fold and smooth down the extra vinyl around the edges.

4 Transfer the photocopied design template onto the vinyl-covered face of the clock. Directions for making a carbon paper transfer are on page 14.

What You Need

Flat glass circle, 9 inches (22.9 cm) in diameter, with a predrilled center hole

Purchased clock movement

Transparent glass spray paints in red, yellow, and blue

Glass cleaner

Paper towels, or a lint-free cloth

Photocopy of design template (page 44) sized to fit your clock

Self-adhesive vinyl in white

Squeegee

Carbon paper

Transparent tape

Craft knife with fixed and swivel blades

Straightedge or ruler

Scissors

Ballpoint pen, or pencil

Cotton-tipped swabs

Pick-out tool (optional)

5 Install the fixed blade into the craft knife. Cut along the straight lines of the numbers using the straightedge or ruler as a guide. Change to the swivel craft knife blade and cut all the curved lines on the numbers.

6 Peel away the vinyl from the clock face, keeping the vinyl squares that surround each number intact. Place the vinyl backing paper over the remaining stencils and flatten them with a squeegee. Clean off any excess adhesive residue with a moist cotton-tipped swab.

7 Read the application procedures and safety precautions recommended by the glass spray-paint manufacturer. Start with the red can of spray paint and the left side of the clock face. Spray in one direction, from top to bottom, using one light, unbroken stroke of paint. Begin the spray slightly above the top edge of the glass and continue spraying slightly past the bottom edge. Spray the red paint approximately two-thirds of the way across the clock face.

8 Change to the blue spray paint and start on the right side of the clock face. Make light strokes from top to bottom, moving about two-thirds of the way across the clock. The blue spray paint will overlap the red spray paint to create a center strip of purple.

9 Spray a thin band of yellow paint from top to bottom along the right edge of the clock face and then along the left edge of the clock face. This will create an orange strip of color on the left edge and a green strip of color on the right edge. Repeat this step to increase opacity and color saturation if desired. Let the spray paint dry, ideally overnight.

10 Insert the pick-out tool or the tip of the craft knife blade under the center of each stencil and lift the vinyl away from the glass. Remove any adhesive residue left on the surface of the glass with a moist cotton-tipped swab.

11 Working from the back of the clock face, feed the post of the clock movement through the hole in the center of the glass. Attach the hands to the post and fasten them in place using the hardware that came with the clock movement. Consult the manufacturer's instructions for the specific assembly procedure. Install a battery into your new clock and set the hands to the correct time.

Etching with Creams and Liquids

Crafters now have an easy, safe, and inexpensive way to transform the surface of glass. New etching creams and liquids produce a frosted, permanent finish in just a few short minutes. The active chemical in this process is ammonium bifluoride, a safer substance than traditional etching acids.

The basic technique of etching with creams and liquids is simple. You expose the surface of the glass to the product (either by spreading or squeezing the cream or dipping the glass into the liquid), wait for approximately 15 minutes, and rinse and dry the glass completely. Every place where the cream or liquid made contact with the glass will be permanently etched. Your finished piece will be food, drink, and dishwasher safe.

A variety of glass items to decorate

Materials

GLASS

Flat glass is an ideal practice surface for the beginning etcher. It's simple to follow a pattern taped underneath flat glass. Stencils cling to this surface with ease. Flat glass responds well to both cream and liquid etching. Curved glass is slightly more challenging only when you apply a stencil resist. It's not recommended to use stencil resists with textured glasses, because their irregular surfaces won't accommodate proper vinyl adhesion. Textured and molded glass surfaces respond far better to liquid etching dips and freehand designs. Etching colored glass can produce beautiful results if the color runs throughout the glass and isn't just a top-coating.

Even on clear glass, some coatings prevent etching creams and liquids from doing their job. If you're unsure, find a small, inconspicuous place to test-etch the glass before creating your design.

RESISTS

Many etched glass projects are created by choosing areas to etch and masking areas to be protected from the etching. Any material that acts as a mask, blocking the etching process, is called a *resist*.

STENCILS

Stencils are a traditional resist. They can be store-bought or custom cut. All you need to make your own stencil is self-adhesive vinyl paper (white works best), a cutting tool (scissors or a craft knife), and a design idea. Both standard stencils and reverse stencils make great resists. The method to use is determined by your composition. Standard stencils leave

Self-adhesive vinyl with paper backing, metal ruler, swivel-blade craft knife, pick-out tool, fixed-blade craft knife, scissors

the glass surrounding the design exposed, while reverse stencils are used to mask the same area. The Starlight Lantern, page 58, uses both stenciling techniques in one project to great effect.

CARBON PAPER TRANSFER

To create your own stencils, you'll need to transfer a pattern from this book or from your own drawing onto self-adhesive vinyl. First, size the pattern to fit the glass. Use a photocopier to reduce or enlarge a design, depending on your needs. Next, place a sheet of self-adhesive vinyl on your work surface with the vinyl surface facing up. Lay a piece of carbon paper over the vinyl with the carbon side facing down. Position your pattern on top of the carbon paper. Secure this carbon transfer "sandwich" in place with tape. Use a ballpoint pen to firmly and evenly trace your design. Peel off the tape and remove the pattern and carbon paper. Your design is now drawn on the vinyl.

CUTTING OUT STENCILS

You can cut out a stencil either before or after adhering the vinyl to the glass. Although there are no solid rules to determine which method to use, certain factors should be considered. Cut out your vinyl stencil before placing it on the glass when you intend to later use the leftover pieces as resists (photo 1), or when you need to see through the stencil to accurately position it on the glass. Apply the vinyl to the glass before cutting out the stencil if you'll be using a swivel blade to cut intricate curves, or if you're working with a large stencil. Whichever method you choose, take care not to cut past the intersection of two pattern lines such as in the points of a triangle or the corners of a square. Etching cream can seep under any small slit in the vinyl, compromising the area you intended to mask.

Photo 1

Photo 2

APPLYING SELF-ADHESIVE VINYL

The process for applying self-adhesive vinyl to glass remains the same regardless of when the pattern is cut.

1. Clean the surface of the glass to remove all price stickers, adhesive residue, dirt, and oil. Under most circumstances, common glass cleaner works well.

2. Peel a corner or edge of the backing paper away from the vinyl.

3. Press the exposed vinyl adhesive onto the glass surface. Work across the glass, peeling away more backing and smoothing down the vinyl with your hand or a squeegee until fully in place (photo 2).

4. Cover the vinyl with a piece of backing paper. Rub the squeegee over the paper to stabilize the edges of the vinyl and remove any wrinkles or air bubbles.

5. Remove any residue that has seeped out from under the edge of the secured stencil with a moist cotton swab.

6. For additional protection, surround the stencil with scrap vinyl extension strips to shield adjoining surface areas from the etching product.

7. Etch the glass as soon as possible. The longer the vinyl is attached to the glass, the more difficult it will be to remove.

SELF-ADHESIVE VINYL PAPER

Self-adhesive vinyl paper is an excellent resist without a cutout design. Strips of vinyl can be arranged in straight-edged and geometric patterns. Practical applications include horizontal and vertical stripes, checkerboard grids, and diamond motifs.

APPLYING SELF-ADHESIVE VINYL RESISTS

To perform this masking technique, follow the same process described above in Applying Self-Adhesive Vinyl. If there are overlapping strips of vinyl, there's one additional step. Burnish all intersecting vinyl seams with a blunt tool or your fingernail to prevent etching cream or liquid from seeping underneath.

RESIST GEL

Resist gel is a liquid masking substance. The viscosity of resist gel enables you to apply it in several ways. Squeeze it directly onto glass from an applicator bottle using a variety of tips, or brush it on to mask large areas. A liquid mask resist is particularly useful on curved glass surfaces where sticking vinyl stencils can be challenging. Resist gel is also effective on small objects and molded glass surfaces.

Resist gel won't affect the surface of your glass. Application mistakes wash off, providing you with a clean slate to begin your design again. Once you have a satisfactory design, let the gel dry completely before proceeding to etch the glass. Depending upon the thickness of the gel, this can take from minutes to hours. Read the manufacturer's recommendations for specific drying times. Generally, resist gels are cloudy when applied and clear when dry. If you're in a hurry, use a hair dryer to speed the process.

Tip

Applying a stencil resist to curved glass is slightly more challenging. You'll have better results if you leave extra room, approximately ¼ inch (6 mm), around the pattern when you cut it out. Cut small v-shaped vents in the excess vinyl that surrounds the pattern, and make gathers as needed for a smooth application.

APPLYING RESIST GEL WITH AN APPLICATOR BOTTLE

Resist gel can be comfortably and precisely dispensed with an applicator bottle and tip. Changeable tips create distinct lines that are thin or bold, wavy or straight, and flat or rounded. On scrap glass or paper, practice applying the gel through an assortment of tips to find the right one for your project. Resist gel has a different consistency than etching cream, and therefore you'll discover varying tip results when switching products. After choosing a tip, squeeze the gel onto the glass as if you're frosting a cake. It's easy to follow pattern lines when using an applicator bottle with resist gel. This technique is marvelous for making small motifs such as dots, leaves, and spirals.

FOUND OBJECTS

Spectacular and imaginative resists are all around you. The natural patterns of leaves and feathers are uniquely handsome. Old trimmings such as lace and doilies also create complex surface textures. Simply use a thin even coating of spray adhesive to adhere your found object to the glass. The resist detaches from the glass when it's washed after etching.

APPLYING FOUND OBJECT RESISTS

1. Clean the glass surface to remove all price stickers, adhesive residue, lint, dirt, and oil.

2. Spray the adhesive on the back side of the object and firmly press the object to the surface of the glass.

3. Cover the attached object with a piece of vinyl backing, and squeegee the surface to secure the bond.

TOOLS

SQUEEGEE

A flexible plastic squeegee is a valuable etching tool. There are two types of useful squeegees. One is T-shaped and spreads etching cream over the surface of exposed glass. The T-shaped squeegee also acts as a device for scraping reusable brands of etching cream back into their containers for future use. A flat, rectangular squeegee assists in adhering self-adhesive vinyl onto glass, rubbing it firmly in place, and ironing out air bubbles and wrinkles. Etching cream could seep underneath the vinyl if wrinkles, bubbles, and insecure edges weren't smoothed out by a squeegee.

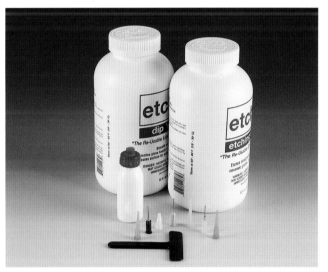

From top: etching liquid, etching cream, applicator bottle, applicator tips, squeegee

APPLICATOR BOTTLES AND TIPS

One quick and easy way to create a design with etching creme or resist gel is to draw it on the glass using an applicator bottle with a changeable tip. A wide assortment of tips are available that produce various line styles. Remember to clean your tips after use. Fill the applicator bottle with warm water, then squeeze the water through the tip. Unblock a clogged tip with a straight pin or needle.

Photo 3

CRAFT KNIFE AND BLADES

To explore etching with stencils, you'll need a good craft knife with a supply of sharp blades. The familiar fixed-blade craft knife is an ideal tool for cutting straight lines. The swivel-blade craft knife rotates 360° when held upright. It helps cut smooth, even edges on curved and rounded stencils. Some craft knives accommodate both types of blades. A special pick-out tool has a sharp edge only on its tip. It's useful for removing the cutout sections of stencils without disturbing the clean and burnished edges around them (photo 3). Substitute the point of your fixed-blade craft knife for a pick-out tool if one isn't available. As for any craft project, remember to have at least one pair of scissors on hand. For cutting some patterns, a sharp pair of scissors is just as effective as a craft knife.

METAL RULER

Having a reliable metal ruler is essential for measuring lengths, drawing straight pattern lines, and making accurate marks directly on the glass. They can also be used as a straightedge to help guide your craft knife.

SAFETY EQUIPMENT

Keep your personal safety in mind anytime you work with chemical compounds. Although etching creams, liquids, and resist gels don't pose any serious dangers, take some general safety precautions.

• Always use etching products in a well-ventilated area.

• Wear a pair of latex gloves when your hands are in direct contact with the creams, liquids, and gels.

• Protect your eyes by wearing a pair of safety goggles if there's any chance of splattering, such as when you dip glass into liquid etch or rinse cream off its surface.

• Wear a safety mask over your nose and mouth during prolonged exposure to etching products to protect yourself from excess fume inhalation.

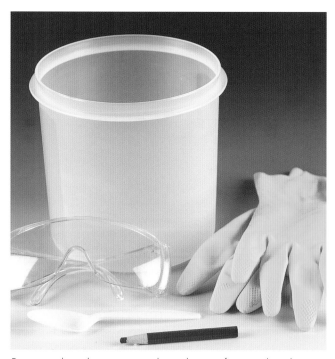

From top: clear plastic container, latex gloves, safety goggles, plastic spoon, china marker

A plastic kitchen cutting board makes a great stencil-cutting surface. It can also act as a rotating base for the glass as you work. Use only a plastic or wooden spoon to stir the etching cream before its application. Partially etching glass in a liquid bath requires a clear plastic container and a water-based marker or china marker. A kitchen timer will help you keep track of the etching process, and you'll need water and a sponge to clean your pieces after they're etched.

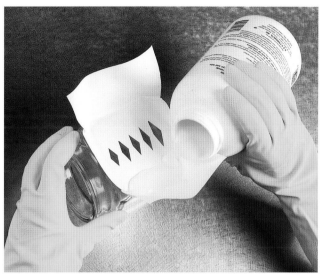

Photo 4

Techniques

APPLYING ETCHING CREAM

There are many ways to apply etching cream onto a glass surface. Use squeegees for even coverage, applicator bottles for small or detailed work, and specialty brushes or tools for decorative effects.

USING A SQUEEGEE

1. Stir the etching cream thoroughly with a wooden or plastic spoon. Cream that has separated produces streaks and an uneven etch.

2. Pour a generous amount of etching cream onto the vinyl near the exposed glass (photo 4). If you're working on a curved surface, build a well out of extra vinyl and place it adjacent to the glass (photo 5). This structure acts as a temporary vessel into which the etching cream can be poured.

Photo 5

3. With the squeegee, pull the cream thickly and evenly across the exposed glass surface (photo 6).

4. Leave the cream on the glass approximately 15 minutes, or for the amount of time suggested by the manufacturer.

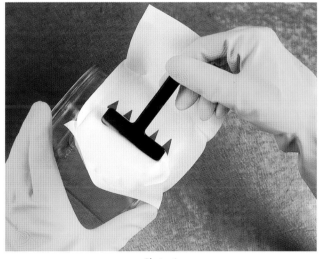

Photo 6

5. Scrape the cream off the glass with the squeegee. Reusable creams may be scraped directly back into their container.

6. Rinse the glass in water to stop the etching process, remove all remaining cream, and loosen the stencil material. Once the glass is totally dry the etching will be visible.

USING AN APPLICATOR BOTTLE

1. Clean the surface of the glass to remove all price stickers, adhesive residue, lint, dirt, and oil. Under most circumstances, common glass cleaner works well.

2. Stir the etching cream with a wooden or plastic spoon. Pour a small amount of cream into an applicator bottle.

3. Select a tip and insert it into the top of the applicator bottle. Test the line of cream on scrap glass or paper. Make sure you're satisfied with your selection. The etching cream begins to alter the surface of the glass immediately upon contact. Once you start making your design, you can't wipe the cream off and begin again.

4. Trace a pattern affixed to the glass (photo 7) or draw a motif by hand (photo 8).

5. Leave the cream on the glass approximately 15 minutes, or for the amount of time suggested by the manufacturer.

6. Rinse the glass in water to stop the etching process, remove all remaining cream, and loosen the stencil material. Once the glass is totally dry the etching will be visible.

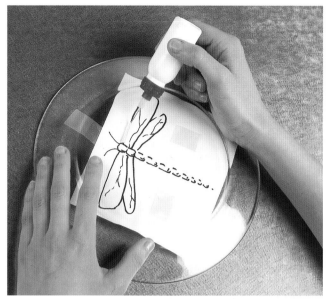

Photo 7

Photo 8

ALTERNATIVE APPLICATORS

Decorative techniques usually associated with painting, such as sponging, brushing, and stamping can add depth and texture to cream etching. To learn the basics of sponging and stamping, see page 16. Brush etching cream onto glass to produce less traditional yet intriguing effects. Although you're encouraged to experiment with different paintbrushes, remember that etching chemicals are stronger than paint and can damage bristles.

USING ETCHING LIQUID

Choose a liquid bath when you want to etch most, if not all, of a glass object. Etching liquids work great on small items, complex curves, and irregular surfaces.

THE TOTAL ETCH

To create a uniformly etched surface, dipping glass into a bath of etching liquid couldn't be more simple.

1. Fill a plastic container with enough etching liquid to cover the object.

2. Place the glass into the etch bath (photo 9). Move the object around gently with a wooden or plastic spoon.

3. Let the glass sit in the bath for the recommended time.

4. Lift the glass out of the bath, rinse it with water, and dry it completely.

THE PARTIAL ETCH

A few preparations need to be made to partially etch a glass surface using the liquid bath method. The desired effect can be well worth the extra effort. First, place the object to be etched into an empty plastic container. Fill the container with water until it reaches the level on the object where the etching

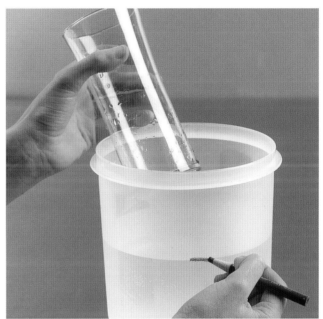
Photo 10

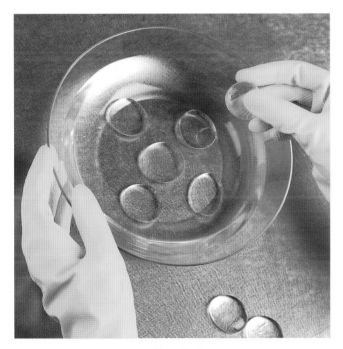
Photo 9

Photo 11

Photo 12

should end. Remove the glass from the plastic container and the water level will drop. Record this level on the outside of the container with a water-based marker or china marker (photo 10). Empty the water out of the container, and dry the inside of the container as well as the object to be etched. Pour etching liquid into the plastic container until you reach the marked level. Place your glass into the etching bath slowly and try to avoid any splashing (photo 11). Don't move the glass once it's resting on the bottom of the container. Allow the glass to stay in the bath approximately 15 minutes, then remove, rinse, and dry.

Tip

After etching in a liquid bath, there may be a small unetched spot left underneath an object, such as a bottle or glass. An air bubble trapped below the surface of the liquid prevented the spot from etching. To eliminate air bubbles, lower glass objects into etch baths at a slight angle. Take care not lower the glass at too great an angle—the glass may etch further than you intended! Unetched spots can be easily remedied after the bath is complete. Simply apply a small amount of etching cream to a gloved finger and rub it on the unetched spot (photo 12). Wait only five minutes, then rinse and dry the spot.

Frost on the Vine Mirror

Designer
DIANA LIGHT

Once you add two etched borders and a graceful vine motif, no one will believe the humble beginnings of this ordinary mirror. A simple self-adhesive vinyl resist shapes the etching, and it's further enhanced by a relief outliner and sparkling silver paint.

What You Do

1 Measure the width of the mirror with the ruler. Place the self-adhesive vinyl on your work surface with the backing paper facing up. Draw a rectangle on the backing paper with a width equal to the glass in the mirror and a height of at least 6 inches (15.2 cm). Cut out the vinyl rectangle with the scissors or craft knife.

2 Measure and mark a straight line that is 2½ inches (6.4 cm) down from the top of the mirror. Peel the backing paper away from one corner of the vinyl. Lightly press the exposed vinyl down on the surface of the mirror below the marked edge. Peel away more backing paper and press down more vinyl a little at a time, working your way across the line. Place the backing paper over the attached vinyl and squeegee across the entire surface to ensure a secure fit. Clean any vinyl residue off the surface of the mirror with a moist cotton-tipped swab. Clean the mirror strip above the vinyl with the glass cleaner and a paper towel or lint-free cloth.

3 Prepare the etching cream. Pour a line of etching cream onto the vinyl under the area to be etched.

4 Use the squeegee to pull the etching cream across the exposed 2½-inch (6.4 cm) strip of mirror. Let the cream etch the glass. After the time has elapsed, remove the cream from the mirror with a damp sponge. Dry the surface thoroughly.

5 Repeat steps 1 through 4 on the bottom edge of the mirror.

What You Need

Full-length mirror

Etching cream

Water-based, air-drying relief outliner in silver

Water-based, air-drying stained glass paint in silver

Glass cleaner

Paper towels, or a lint-free cloth

Photocopy of design template sized to fit your mirror (page 57)

Self-adhesive vinyl in white

Squeegee

Carbon paper

Transparent tape

Plastic applicator bottle

Small applicator tip

Craft knife, or scissors

Ruler

Ballpoint pen, or pencil

Straight pin

Cotton-tipped swabs

Sponge

Water

6 Transfer the photocopied design template onto the top etched glass strip. Directions for making this carbon paper transfer are on page 14.

7 Turn the template upside down and transfer it to the etched area at the bottom of the mirror.

8 On the scrap glass or paper, practice outlining with the tube of silver paint. For a description of different outlining techniques, see page 15. Apply the lines of outliner paint on top of the carbon transfer design. Complete this step for both the top and the bottom of the mirror. Allow the paint to dry. Outlining mistakes can be scraped off the mirror with the tip of the craft knife.

9 Prepare the silver stained glass paint and pour some into the plastic applicator bottle. Insert the small applicator tip into the top of the bottle and make a tight seal. On the scrap flat glass or paper, practice painting with the applicator bottle. Fill in the outlines of the leaves and the circles with silver paint. Use a straight pin to pop any bubbles that appear in the paint. Wipe away any paint from on top of the outliner with a moist cotton-tipped swab. Complete this step for both etched strips on the mirror. Let the silver paint dry.

Starlight Lantern

Designer
DIANA LIGHT

THIS PROJECT MAKES THE
MOST OF A SINGLE STENCIL
PATTERN. FIRST, A STANDARD
STENCIL SCATTERS ETCHED
STARS ALL OVER ONE PANEL
OF YOUR LANTERN. THEN,
THE CUTOUT SHAPES FROM
THE FIRST STENCIL BECOME
REVERSE STENCILS, CREATING
CLEAR STARS FLOATING ON
AN ETCHED BACKGROUND
ON THE NEXT PANEL. WHEN
ALL THE PANELS ARE ETCHED,
YOU'LL HAVE A LANTERN THAT
REALLY SHINES.

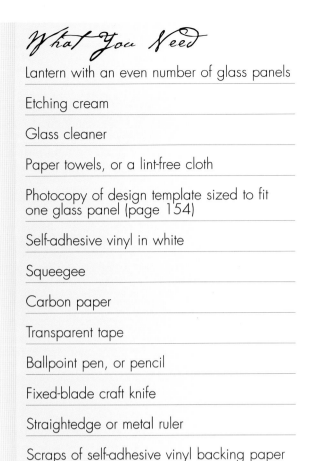

What You Need

Lantern with an even number of glass panels

Etching cream

Glass cleaner

Paper towels, or a lint-free cloth

Photocopy of design template sized to fit one glass panel (page 154)

Self-adhesive vinyl in white

Squeegee

Carbon paper

Transparent tape

Ballpoint pen, or pencil

Fixed-blade craft knife

Straightedge or metal ruler

Scraps of self-adhesive vinyl backing paper

What You Do

1 Transfer the photocopied design template onto the self-adhesive vinyl. Directions for making a carbon paper transfer are on page 47. Transfer the pattern once for every two panels in your lantern. Mark the corners of the stencils according to the measurements of your lantern's panels, then leave a border of self-adhesive vinyl measuring 1 ½ to 2 inches (3.8 to 5 cm) beyond the marked corners.

2 With a sharp blade in your craft knife, cut out the star shapes in each stencil, being careful not to overcut at any of the points on the star. (Remember, you'll be using both the star shapes and the standard stencil; both need to be cleanly cut.)

3 Begin peeling off the self-adhesive vinyl backing paper on one end of the stencil, and position that end on one of the lantern panels using the corners you marked in step 1 as a guide. Once you're sure of the stencil's position, continue peeling off the backing paper, and use the squeegee to guide the stencil into position. To press the stencil firmly in place and remove any air bubbles, cover it with a scrap of self-adhesive vinyl backing and run the squeegee over it.

4 Wipe off any adhesive residue the vinyl may have left on the glass. Add extension strips of self-adhesive vinyl around the stencil's border, then pinch the strips at the corners to make a well for the etching cream. Pour a small amount of cream into the well and pull it smoothly over the stencil area with the squeegee. Let the cream etch the glass. When the time has elapsed remove the cream, detach the stencil as you rinse the panel with water, and dry the panel.

5 On the next panel, stick the cutout stars into position using the stencil as a guide. Cover the panel with a scrap of self-adhesive vinyl backing paper, and run the squeegee over the stars to remove any air bubbles and ensure that they're firmly in place. Wipe off any adhesive residue on the glass.

6 Cut a strip of self-adhesive vinyl a bit longer than the panel and approximately 1 ½ to 2 inches (3.8 to 5 cm) wide and attach it to one side of the panel you're about to etch (attach the vinyl to the lantern material rather than the glass). Pour a line of etching cream onto the strip and pull it over the stencil area with the squeegee. Let the cream etch the glass, scrape it off, and remove the stars as you rinse the panel with water. Dry the panel. Repeat the alternating process on all of the lantern's remaining panels.

Bamboo Coasters

Designer

DIANA LIGHT

A TROPICAL IMAGE FORMS WHEN YOU ARRANGE THESE FUNCTIONAL AND ATTRACTIVE COASTERS INTO A FOUR-SQUARE GRID. ETCHING ON BOTH SIDES OF THE GLASS EXTENDS THE DEPTH OF THE COMPOSITION AND GIVES YOU AN OPPORTUNITY TO REFINE YOUR CREAM APPLICATION SKILLS ON AN EASY FLAT SURFACE.

What You Do

1 Visit your local glass supplier and have four flat glass squares custom cut to the measurements specified above. Ask the glazier to polish all edges of the cut glass for safe handling.

2 Clean both surfaces of each glass piece with the glass cleaner and a paper towel or lint-free cloth. Place one piece of glass over each of the four elements of the photocopied design template. Use rolled tubes of transparent tape to secure the glass pieces to the template.

3 Mix the etching cream and pour some into a plastic applicator bottle. Attach a large applicator tip to the top of the bottle and make a tight seal. On the scrap glass or paper, practice using the applicator bottle with the etching cream.

4 With the etching cream draw over all the bamboo stalks in the design pattern on

What You Need

4 pieces custom-cut flat glass, each 4 x 4 x ⅛ to ³⁄₁₆ inches (10.2 x 10.2 x .3 to 2.1 cm)

Etching cream

Glass cleaner

Paper towels, or a lint-free cloth

Photocopy of design template (below) sized to fit your glass

Plastic applicator bottle

Large and small applicator tips

Transparent tape

16 clear plastic self-adhesive picture frame bumpers

Water

Sponge

Towels

Scrap flat glass or paper

each of the four coasters. Allow the cream to etch the glass. When the time has elapsed, use a damp sponge to remove all etching cream from each coaster, then dry each coaster with a towel.

5 Replace the large applicator tip with the small tip. Fill in all the bamboo leaves on all four coasters. Let the cream etch the glass. When the time has elapsed, remove the glass pieces from the template and rinse the coasters under running water to remove the etching cream. Dry each coaster with a towel.

6 On top of the template, rearrange the four pieces of glass into the mirror image of their original composition with the unetched side of the glass facing up. The coasters that were on the left are now on the right. The coasters that were on the right are now on the left. Their top and bottom orientation remains the same. Use pieces of transparent tape to secure the glass pieces to the template.

7 Repeat steps 4 and 5 on each glass coaster.

8 Attach the small tip to the applicator bottle of etching cream. Follow the photocopied design template to draw the dragonfly on each coaster. Draw two dragonflies on the front side of opposite coasters (lower left and upper right), and two dragonflies on the back side of opposite coasters (lower right and upper left). Let the cream etch the glass. Rinse and dry the coasters.

9 Adhere one clear plastic picture frame bumper under each corner of all four coasters.

Glamorous Panorama

Designer
DIANA LIGHT

DRESS UP THE PRESENTATION OF YOUR MOST TREASURED PHOTOGRAPHS WITH THESE CURLING CORNER MOTIFS. THE ELEGANT DESIGN IS SIMPLE TO TRANSFER. BEST OF ALL, THIS FLEXIBLE ETCHING ACCENT ALSO FITS STANDARD-SIZE PICTURE FRAMES.

What You Do

1 Remove the glass from the picture frame. Place the self-adhesive vinyl on your work surface with the backing paper facing up. Put the glass on top of the backing paper near its edge. Trace around the glass with the pencil or ballpoint pen. Cut along the marked lines to produce a piece of self-adhesive vinyl that fits the dimensions of the glass.

2 Clean the surface of the glass with glass cleaner and a paper towel or lint-free cloth.

3 Peel one corner of backing paper away from the self-adhesive vinyl cut in step 1. Lightly press down the exposed vinyl in one corner of the picture frame glass. Peel more backing paper away and press the vinyl down a little at a time. Use a squeegee to smooth out any air bubbles.

4 Transfer the photocopied design template onto one corner of the glass. Directions for making a carbon paper transfer are on page 47. Repeat this process for all four corners of the picture frame glass.

5 With a fixed-blade craft knife, cut out all the straight lines of the pattern. Exchange the blade in the craft knife. With a swivel blade, cut out all the curved lines. Extract the cutout design with a pick-out tool or with the end of the fixed-blade craft knife. Lift the vinyl from the center of the cutout to avoid damaging the stencil's edge.

6 Cover the picture frame glass with backing paper. Reinforce the vinyl stencil with the squeegee. Wipe away any adhesive residue left on the glass with a moist cotton-tipped swab.

7 Prepare the etching cream. Carefully pour the cream directly onto the vinyl-covered glass near one of the stencil cutouts. Pull the etching cream thickly

What You Need

Picture frame glass

Etching cream

Glass cleaner

Paper towels, or a lint-free cloth

Photocopy of design template (below) sized to fit your glass

Self-adhesive vinyl in white

Squeegee

Carbon paper

Transparent tape

Ballpoint pen, or pencil

Craft knife with fixed and swivel blades

Straightedge or metal ruler

Cotton-tipped swabs

Sponge

Water

Towel

Pick-out tool, optional

and evenly across the stencil with the squeegee. Repeat this process for the three remaining corners. Allow the cream to etch the glass.

8 With the vinyl still attached, rinse the picture frame glass under running water. Remove the vinyl from the glass and towel dry. Clean the glass again before placing it into the frame.

Double Bubbly

Designer

DIANA LIGHT

CREATE A SPARKLING EVENING FOR TWO WITH A CUSTOMIZED BOTTLE OF CHAMPAGNE AND MATCHING FLUTES. USE RESIST GEL AND ETCHING LIQUID TO ADD A QUICK YET PERSONAL DESIGN TO ALL YOUR GLASS BOTTLES. YOUR EXTRA EFFORT IS SURE TO MAKE A BIG IMPRESSION.

What You Do

CHAMPAGNE BOTTLE

1 Remove all labels from the champagne bottle but leave the foil around the cork intact. Place the champagne bottle in the clear plastic container. Fill the container with water to the height you wish to etch the champagne bottle. Remove the bottle from the plastic container. Mark the water level on the outside of the plastic container with the water-based marker or china marker. Pour the water out of the plastic container, and dry the container thoroughly. Wash and dry the champagne bottle.

2 Transfer the photocopied design templates onto the bottle. Directions for making this carbon paper transfer are on page 14. The complete design for the champagne bottle is two lengths of the bubble template.

3 Mix the resist gel and pour some into a plastic applicator bottle. Attach a small applicator tip to the top of the bottle and make a tight seal. On the scrap glass or paper, practice using the applicator bottle and tip with the resist gel. Squeeze the resist gel from the applicator bottle onto the champagne bottle following the transferred design. Allow the resist gel to dry.

4 Cover a level work surface with newspaper. Put on the safety glasses and the latex gloves. Pour the etching liquid into the plastic container until you reach the line marked in step 1.

5 Lower the champagne bottle into the etching liquid slowly and at a slight angle. Stand the bottle straight up in the etching liquid once it reaches the bottom of the plastic container. Allow the liquid to etch the bottle.

What You Need

Glass champagne bottle

2 glass champagne flutes

Etching cream

Etching liquid

Resist gel

Photocopy of design template sized to fit your bottle and flutes (page 67)

Plastic applicator bottle

Applicator tips

Carbon paper

Transparent tape

Clear plastic container, larger than the champagne bottle

Ballpoint pen, or pencil

Water-based marker, or china marker

Scrap flat glass or paper

Safety goggles

Latex gloves

Water

Towel

6 Once the etching time has elapsed, remove the champagne bottle from the etching liquid, rinse the bottle with water, detach the resist gel, and dry the bottle thoroughly with a towel.

1 Secure the photocopied design template in place on the inside surface of the champagne flutes with pieces of the transparent tape or round beans or grains. Clean the outside surface of the flutes with glass cleaner and a paper towel or lint-free cloth.

2 Mix the resist gel and pour some into the plastic applicator bottle. Attach a small applicator tip to the top of the bottle and make a tight seal. Following the design template, use the resist gel to draw the reflection curve inside each bubble. Allow the resist gel to dry.

3 Mix the etching cream, pour some into a clean plastic applicator bottle, and attach a large applicator tip. On the scrap glass or paper, practice using the applicator bottle with the etching cream. With the template as your guide, squeeze the etching cream out of the applicator bottle and over the reflection curves to create the bubble shapes.

4 Let the cream etch the glass. Rinse the flutes with water and dry them completely.

5 To etch the stem of the champagne flute, first fill the flute with water and place it in the clear plastic container. Fill the container with water to the height where the stem of the flute meets the base of the flute's cup. Remove the champagne flute from the clear plastic container, and mark the water level on the outside of the container. Pour the water out of the plastic container. Dry the champagne flute and the container.

6 Wearing latex gloves and safety glasses, pour the etching liquid into the plastic container to the level marked in step 5. Lower the stem of the champagne flute into the etching liquid slowly and at a very slight angle. Stand the flute straight up in the etching liquid once the foot of the flute reaches the bottom of the plastic container. Let the liquid etch the glass.

7 Once the etching time has elapsed, gently remove the champagne flute from the liquid. Rinse the flute with water, then dry the flute completely. If it's reusable, pour the etching liquid from the plastic container back into its original bottle.

8 If there's a small unetched spot under the bottom of the champagne bottle or the flutes it means that an air bubble was trapped during the etching process. See page 54 for further instructions.

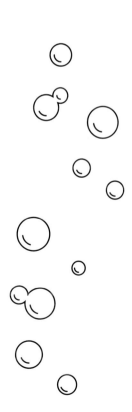

ETCHING GLASS

Fairy Bath Oil Bottles

Designer
DIANA LIGHT

LET THESE DELIGHTFUL PIXIES CAST THEIR RELAXING SPELL AS YOU SLIP INTO AN AROMATIC BATH. THE SILHOUETTES ARE MASKED WITH A GEL RESIST BEFORE THE BOTTLES TAKE A DIP IN ETCHING LIQUID. MAKE EXTRAS FOR YOUR FRIENDS, AND SPREAD THE MAGIC.

What You Need

2 glass bath oil bottles with glass stoppers

Etching liquid

Resist gel

Photocopy of design templates sized to fit your bottles (page 70)

Plastic applicator bottle

Small applicator tip

Clear plastic container larger than the glass bottles with stoppers in place

Carbon paper

Water-based marker, or china marker

Wooden or plastic spoon

Ballpoint pen, or pencil

Scrap flat glass or paper

Safety goggles

Latex gloves

Cotton-tipped swabs

Water

Towels

What You Do

1 Fill one bath oil bottle with water to give it additional weight. Seal the water in the bottle with the stopper. Place the bottle in the clear plastic container. Fill the container with water to the top of the bottle stopper. Remove the glass bottle from the plastic container. Mark the water level on the outside of the plastic container. Pour the water out of the plastic container, and dry it thoroughly. Wash and dry the glass bottle.

2 Use pieces of transparent tape or round beans or grains to secure the photocopied template on the inside of the bottle. Another option is to transfer the drawing to the outside of the bottle with carbon paper. Directions for making this carbon-paper transfer are on page 14.

3 Pour the resist gel into the plastic applicator bottle. Fit the applicator bottle with a small tip and form a tight seal. On the scrap of flat glass or paper, practice using the resist gel with the applicator bottle and tip. Carefully trace the contour of the design on the bottle, then fill in the outline with resist gel. If you transferred the template using carbon paper, be sure the resist gel completely covers the carbon lines. Exposed carbon resists the etching liquid but won't leave a smooth line. Let the resist gel dry.

4 Cover a level work surface with newspaper. Put on the safety glasses and latex gloves. Pour the etching liquid into the plastic container until you reach the line marked in step 1.

5 Fill the bath oil bottle with water and tightly engage the stopper. Lower the bottle into the etching liquid slowly and at a slight angle. Stand the bottle straight up in the etching liquid once it reaches the bottom of the plastic container.

6 Let the liquid etch the bottle. Then, remove the bottle from the etching liquid, rinse the bottle with water, detach the resist gel, and dry the bottle thoroughly with a towel. If it's reusable, pour the etching liquid back into its container. Remove the mark made on the plastic container.

7 Repeat steps 1 through 6 to etch the second bath oil bottle.

Stained Glass

This uniquely rewarding craft is much easier than you might think. There are only three steps to creating beautiful stained glass. First, glass must be scored and broken. Next, it must be assembled with lead came or copper foil. Finally, the joints or seams are soldered together. It's just that simple!

The stained glass projects in this book are designed expressly for the beginner, and they're explained in a clear, step-by-step process. With their practical scale and limited number of glass pieces, these projects provide a great introduction to the pleasures of stained glass.

A variety of stained glass and stained glass accessories

Materials

STAINED GLASS

Your first visit to a stained glass supplier may be overwhelming as there are so many wonderful glasses. Fortunately, there are trained specialists to assist you in selecting the glass that corresponds to both your taste and skill level. Your supplier wants you to have a long, happy, and productive experience working with stained glass. They know which glasses are easier to work with and are happy to make recommendations. Since all of the projects in this book were created with the beginner in mind, the designers selected glasses that are widely available and, most importantly, simple to use.

Most commercial stained glasses are machine made. The fundamental ingredients that combine to make glass are silica sand, soda ash, and lime. These elements are heated to high temperatures to transform them into a molten or liquid state. Molten glass is poured onto a metal surface and gradually cooled into sheets. There are many varieties of machine-made glass, and they're the best (and least expensive) choice for the beginning stained glass artist.

Antique glass is the category of stained glass that's not machine made.

Cathedral glass is the category of all machine-made stained glass. Because of its even surface texture, it's easy to cut. Ideal for beginners.

Glue chip glass is a translucent glass that has a frosty pattern on its surface.

Iridescent glass is cathedral glass thinly coated with metallic salts to produce a shimmer.

Opalescent glass is the name for glasses that aren't transparent. These opaque glasses come in many colors and textures.

Semi-antique glass is a transparent glass that's consistent in color and thickness but has a surface pattern of thin, narrow grooves. Despite its texture, semi-antique glass remains an excellent type for beginners.

Streaky glass is created from two or more colors of cathedral glass swirled, but not blended, together on one sheet.

Water glass appears to have a wavy texture although its surface is even and smooth.

STAINED GLASS ACCESSORIES

Roundels are smooth-edged circles of glass. Roundels are sold in many sizes and colors. They can be machine-pressed or handmade.

Bevels are preformed, beveled-edged glass shapes available in different shapes and sizes. Usually clear or soft-colored, light sparkles through beveled edges to create special effects.

Cluster is an arrangement of bevels made into a set.

Nuggets resemble a glass marble with one flat side. Nuggets come in many colors and sizes.

LEAD CAME

Leaded stained glass is the most familiar variety. A panel of leaded stained glass is assembled with lead came. Came is a slender, grooved lead bar

Clockwise from bottom right: solder, soldering irons, soldering iron stand, flux remover, acetone, copper foil tape, liquid flux, paste flux, H-channel lead came, U-channel zinc came, lead vise, horseshoe nails

that holds pieces of stained glass together. It also provides the linear outline for the design. Lead came is generally sold in 4- and 6-foot (1.2 and 1.8 m) lengths. It can be cut to any size with lead nippers or bent to different angles. The two basic channel profiles of lead came are U-shaped, used for framing, and H-shaped, used to hold the interior pieces of stained glass. The H shape allows one piece of glass to slide into each side of the channel. The came's core is the small portion of lead that lies at the center of the channel—the horizontal line that crosses the H. It's almost always $\frac{1}{16}$ inch (1.6 mm) thick. For this reason, the design lines in leaded stained glass patterns are usually $\frac{1}{16}$ inch (1.6 mm) wide. Lead came must always be stretched before using. Place one end of the length of came into a lead vise. Grip the opposite end of the came with pliers. Brace yourself for safety while you pull until the lead is straight and firm.

COPPER FOIL

To make a piece of copper foiled stained glass, each piece of cut glass is ground or sanded to fit a pattern, then wrapped with a self-adhesive strip of copper foil. The copper foil acts as a foundation for the solder that ultimately joins the project. Copper foil stained glass only uses lengths of came for framing. Copper foil is commonly sold in 36-yard (32.4 m) rolls and in several widths. Wider foil produces wider seams between stained glass pieces. The copper foil recommended for beginning stained glass artists is $\frac{7}{32}$-inch (55 mm) wide. It's simple to apply, covers most glass edges, and provides appealing results. Foil tapes can be copper-colored on both sides or have a black or silver backing. One roll of copper foil tape accommodates many projects. Keep it fresh by storing it in a zip-top plastic bag.

TOOLS

PATTERN SHEARS

Pattern shears look like scissors but they actually have three blades. Pattern shears are used to cut out the interior lines of a stained glass template. As they cut, pattern shears trim a thin strip of paper around the pattern line (photo 1). This gap signifies the distance between the glass pieces that will later be filled by the copper foil or the lead came's core. Keep the pattern shears perpendicular to the design template when cutting out pattern pieces. Use the inner part of the blade, and cut in short strokes. Discard the small shavings of paper from the shears as you work.

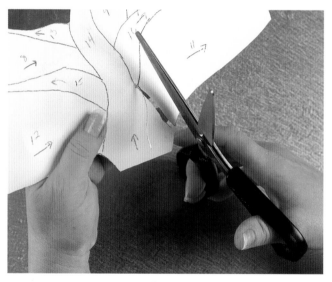

Photo 1

GLASS CUTTER

Most manual glass cutters operate on the same principle. A metal wheel rotates as it's pushed across a piece of glass. The wheel's sharp edge creates a tiny scratch on the glass called a *score*. There are many varieties to chose from, but a simple steel-wheel glass cutter works fine for the beginner. The more complex (and costly) tools feature comfort grips and self-lubrication.

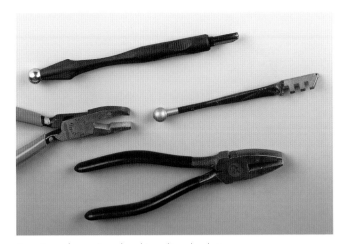

From top: glass cutters, breaking pliers, lead nippers

BREAKING PLIERS

Breaking pliers have smooth jaws that firmly grip glass without scratching it. The main function of breaking pliers is to break glass along the score line created by a glass cutter (photo 2). They're also useful hand extensions when you're working with glass pieces too small to grip comfortably. This role makes having two pairs of breaking pliers a good idea.

Photo 2

GROZING PLIERS

Grozing pliers have serrated jaws. They work like teeth to nibble away tiny fragments from the edges of cut glass. One side of the pliers is straight and one side is curved. Use the straight side of the pliers to snap off larger pieces. To shear off tiny slivers from the edges of the glass, close the rounded and serrated interior jaws gently, then roll the pliers downwards (photo 3). This process is called *grozing* and it should always be performed over a large trash can.

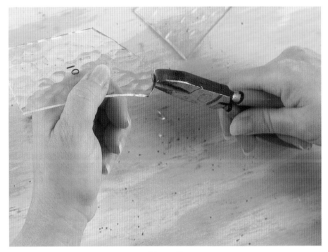

Photo 3

LEAD NIPPERS

Lead nippers cut the came for stained glass projects. They're flush-cutting pliers, similar to wire cutters but with only one flat side. Always use the flat side of the lead nippers to cut the came for your projects (photo 4). The other side is angled, therefore every cut produces a point on the leftover lead (photo 5).

Photo 4

Photo 5

The pointed side must be removed prior to cutting your next piece of lead. Fortunately, these scrap pieces are recycled and play a valuable role. They become the bumpers that hold your glass in place during assembly.

HACKSAW

Metals that are too rigid to be cut with lead nippers, such as zinc came and brass hanging rods, are easily cut with a hacksaw.

HORSESHOE NAILS

Horseshoe nails are flat-sided and hold leaded glass pieces and bumpers in place while a panel is being assembled. The flat side of the nail is installed flush with the outer edge of the bumper or came. If you pull horseshoe nails out of your work board by rocking them side to side, they're reusable.

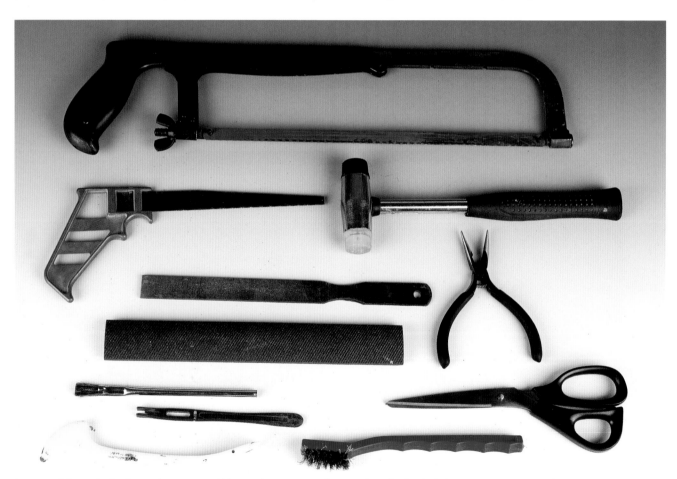

From top, left to right: hacksaws, hammer, metal file, grinding stone, needle-nose pliers, flux brush, foil crimper, pattern sheers, foil burnisher, wire brush

HAMMER

A small hammer is essential for driving horseshoe nails. You'll also tack a design pattern and template paper to your work surface prior to making a carbon paper transfer. Hammers with plastic or rubber heads are also available. They drive nails and can be used to tap stained glass pieces into place inside the channel of came.

WIRE BRUSH

Lead came must be thoroughly cleaned before it's fluxed and soldered because it oxidizes quickly and solder won't adhere to oxidized lead. Use a wire brush to clean all lead joints before soldering (photo 6). Wire brushes are easily obtained from a stained glass supplier.

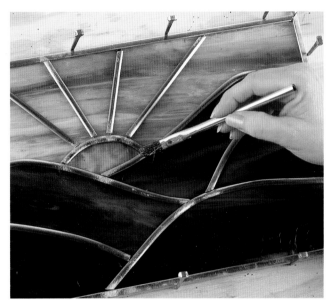
Photo 7

after you finish soldering. Flux will oxidize lead and copper and can discolor stained glass if left on the surface. If you're working with liquid flux, use a commercial flux remover with a damp paper towel, cloth, or cotton ball to remove the excess (photo 8). Use acetone with a cotton ball to remove excess paste flux. Read and follow the manufacturer's instructions and safety precautions when working with these chemicals.

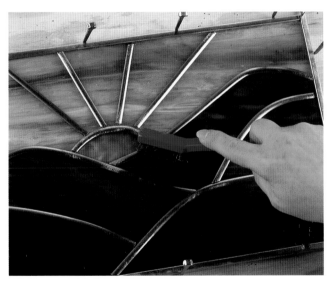
Photo 6

FLUX

Flux is a chemical that must be brushed onto metals before soldering (photo 7). Flux loosens the oxides on the surface of metals, such as lead, copper, and zinc enabling the solder to flow evenly and bond well. Flux is sold in both a liquid and paste form. All flux must be cleaned off your project immediately

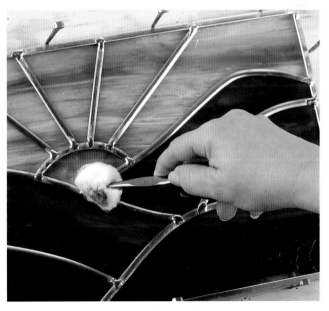
Photo 8

SOLDERING IRON

A soldering iron distributes solder, the material that holds stained glass together. The iron is wand-shaped and consists of a heat-resistant handle fitted with a replaceable ¼ or ⅜ inch (6 or 9.5 mm) tip. The recommended temperature range for a stained glass soldering iron is 900° F (500° C) for lead projects, and 1000° F (537° C) for copper foil projects, regardless of wattage. Most soldering irons come with a tray to hold a damp natural sponge, cotton rag, or wire tip cleaner. You'll want to clean the hot tip of the iron by wiping it on this sponge or rag as you work. Direct heat from the soldering iron should never be touched to anything but the solder wire and the wet sponge or rag. The high temperature of the iron can easily burn the skin and is a fire hazard. Always return your soldering iron to its stand when not in use. Soldering irons can be purchased from stained glass suppliers.

Right to left from top: Finishing compound, patinas, lamp base, hanging wire, hanging loops

PATINAS

Patinas are applied to a completed stained glass panel to alter the appearance of its solder (photo 9). Metallic silver solder lines can be given a black or copper tone with the help of patinas. Read and follow the manufacturer's instructions and safety precautions when working with these chemicals.

Photo 9

Techniques

CREATING A WORK SPACE

You can create stained glass on any steady table that has an even surface. If you don't have a workbench that you can tack nails into, you'll need a thick, rigid piece of wood or plywood to act as your assembly surface. Cover your tabletop with plenty of newspaper to protect its surface. Always keep a dustpan and broom nearby, and sweep up glass slivers frequently.

MAKING TEMPLATES

A leaded glass project requires one photocopied template enlarged to scale. Place the sized design under the glass, and trace around the individual pieces with a permanent marker. Be sure to number each pattern piece on the surface of the glass and add directional arrows as needed. A light table is useful for tracing pattern pieces through dark-colored glass.

You'll need two copies of each copper-foil design you intend to create. One will be the design template from this book, photocopied and enlarged to scale. The second will produce sectional pattern pieces cut from a carbon paper transfer. These pat-

Photo 10

tern pieces are made from heavyweight paper and represent each glass piece in the design. The pattern pieces should be numbered and labeled to reflect glass color and direction (photo 10).

To transfer a design, you'll need a sheet of carbon paper and a sheet of heavyweight paper, such as poster board, to act as your pattern paper. Lay the pattern paper on top of your work surface. Place the carbon paper on top with the carbon side fac-

ing the pattern paper. Position the stained glass design template on top of the carbon paper. Use a hammer and horseshoe nails to stabilize this paper sandwich by tacking it to your work surface in all four corners. Once it's secure, trace around all pattern lines with a ballpoint pen. Number the pattern pieces at this time, put arrows to indicate direction where needed, and make any additional notes. Remove two adjacent horseshoe nails from your work surface, lift up a corner of the design, and double-check that you didn't miss any lines or numbers (photo 11). After a successful transfer, remove

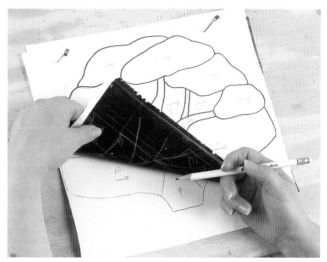

Photo 11

Photo 12

the remaining two nails. Cut out the outer edge of the design template with scissors. Use pattern shears to cut out the individual pattern pieces. Leave plenty of room between pattern pieces when you place them on top of the glass to be traced (photo 12). You'll want to be able to cut the glass directly from edge to edge.

CUTTING GLASS

Cutting glass is much easier that it first seems. Begin by practicing your technique on window glass scraps. Window glass is readily available, thin, and breaks easily. It takes time to find the right amount of pressure to apply to your cutter in order to achieve a proper score.

HOLDING A GLASS CUTTER

To hold a glass cutter correctly, place it between your first and second finger with the cutting wheel facing you. Position your thumb on the front-facing flat hold, and place your first and second fingertips on the back of the thumb rest (photo 13). This keeps the handle vertical and gives you control of where the cutting wheel moves. Cup your second hand lightly and place it over and around the cutter. Rest

Photo 13

your thumb on the top of the cutter. This thumb position provides the downward pressure you need to score the glass.

SCORING THE GLASS

The glass cutter creates a score that weakens the glass so it can be broken cleanly. To break glass into the desired shape, a line is scored that extends from one edge of the glass to another.

Photo 14

• Tidy your work surface before scoring glass.

• Clean the glass with glass cleaner and a paper towel or lint-free cloth.

• Keep the cutting wheel perpendicular to the glass. Scores made with a tilted cutting wheel either break at an angle or fail to break along the entire score.

• Start the score at one edge (photo 14) and continue with it through to the other edge.

• Apply even pressure to the cutter as you pull it across the glass or the score line may be irregular in depth and the glass may not break evenly.

• Keep the cutter's speed consistent along the length of the score.

• As you score the glass, you should hear a soft hissing sound, not a loud rasp. You should also see a barely visible line in the cutter's wake. If that line is white and powdery, or if glass chips fly as you push the cutter, you're applying excessive pressure.

• Never score the same place twice. If your first score line isn't deep enough, score a second line parallel to your first. Break the glass on the second score line, and recycle the side with the bad score. Rolling over an existing score damages the cutting wheel and causes an improper break.

• Lubricate and clean the wheel of your cutter before every score by wiping it across an oil-soaked rag. Even self-lubricating cutters should be wiped to remove glass chips.

BREAKING THE GLASS

Once the glass is scored, it's ready to be separated. You'll know if you've applied the correct scoring pressure once you're ready to break the glass. To break the glass, place both hands on the bottom

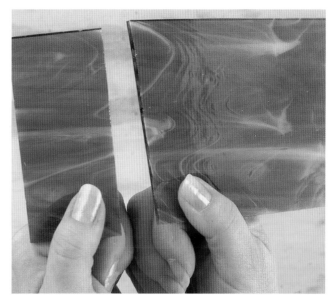

Photo 16

edge of the glass. Position one hand on each side of the score line (photo 15). Place your thumbs on the top surface of the glass and your index-finger knuckles on the bottom surface of the glass. Grip the glass firmly, and pull each hand downward and apart at the same time with the same amount of pressure (photo 16). Your score line should create a fissure that allows the glass to break apart. Practice this technique until you're comfortable with the process and your lines are breaking to your satisfaction. Some glass breaks more easily than others. With experience you'll recognize how different types of glass behave when scored and broken.

SCORING AND BREAKING CURVES

All sorts of shapes can be cut from stained glass. Cutting straight lines and square pieces are easy, end-to-end procedures. Cutting shallow curves requires a small, simple variation in the process. Deep curves or S-shaped curves involve several cuts. Trimming a stained glass piece a little at a time into more manageable pieces helps you cut deeply curved lines and other unconventional shapes.

Photo 15

To cut a shallow curve, position the line of the curve as vertically in front of you as possible. Place your feet parallel to each other and about 10 inches (25.4 cm) apart. Lean on one foot at the top of the curve, pulling the glass cutter straight towards you. Shift your weight to the other foot to complete scoring the curve. Keep the cutter and your arms as perpendicular as possible to the point on the line you're cutting. Score the line by moving your shoulders and whole body rather than moving your wrists or elbows. This method gives you excellent control and accuracy.

GRINDING EDGES

Smoothing the sharp edges of cut glass is a fundamental step in copper foil projects. Carbide grinding stones are a manual way to smooth the edges of glass either under running water or by dipping the stone frequently in water (photo 17). Electric stained glass grinders are diamond-bit routers with a built-in water reservoir. When using a glass grinder, keep the reservoir filled with enough water to keep the edge of the glass wet. Always wear safety goggles when grinding glass. After grinding, dry each glass piece with a towel and renumber any pieces that have lost their markings.

Photo 17

BASIC LEADING

Once all the glass pieces for your project are cut, you'll connect them using lengths of lead or zinc came, then solder each joint to hold the panel together. All components are assembled like a jig-saw puzzle. The glass pieces either fit into U-channel came (for the perimeter edges only) or H-channel came (for all interior edges). For your convenience, each pattern piece in this book has a number (photo 18). This number indicates the easiest sequence of

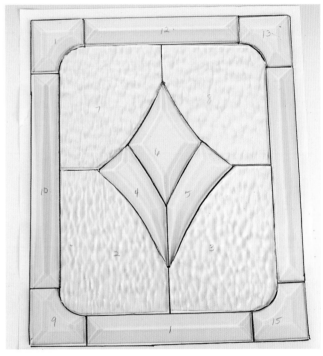

Photo 18

assembly. Following these numbers in order from lowest to highest helps you put your panel together smoothly. Wherever possible, use a larger piece of lead came and curve it over or around two or more glass pieces at once to create a more flowing line. This is an especially useful technique on the curved portions of the Tulip Bravado design on page 91. Always secure the edges of free-moving glass pieces with lead or zinc bumpers, and all strips of lead came with horseshoe nails (photo 19). This

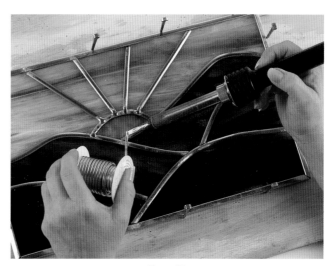

prevents the panel pieces from shifting while you work. Horseshoe nails and bumpers are an integral part of constructing leaded glass. They hold everything in place, level and square, while you work. Remove the horseshoe nails only when you're ready to install a new length of came or section of glass. Where two sections of lead came meet, miter their edges so they'll fit together rather than overlap. U-channel zinc came, ¼ inch wide (6 mm), is the framing material for each project in this book. Always use zinc bumpers to secure glass pieces that will eventually be framed with zinc. In similar fashion, only use lead bumpers to hold spaces for lead came.

SOLDERING

Soldering is the art of joining pieces of glass or came together where they meet. Stained glass solder is solid metal wire melted by the heat of a soldering iron. On leaded projects, solder holds pieces of came together at their joints. On copper foil projects, solder completely covers the foiled seams. Stained glass solder usually comes on 1 pound (.5 kg) spools. Melted solder sticks only to metal surfaces that are clean and fluxed. If solder

drips onto stained glass, it's easily removed once completely cool.

SOLDERING CAME JOINTS

Clean and flux the points to be soldered. Hold the end of the solder wire over the joint of the came and melt a small amount of solder with the iron (photo 20). Apply the melted solder to the joint (photo 21). Once you see the solder touch the lead, lift the iron straight up. If you lift the iron too fast, the solder will only ball up on top of the joint. If you lift the iron too slowly the solder will melt into the crack of the joint or even melt the lead came. If the iron is too hot, the solder will fall off before you can get it to the panel. Wipe the tip of the iron on a wet sponge to cool. Make the solder joints smooth and slightly rounded. Ideally, they should extend in each direction for a distance equal to the width of the came. Corner solder joints are L-shaped. Where three pieces of came intersect, the solder joints are T- or Y-shaped.

COPPER FOIL ASSEMBLY

Copper foiling projects often have more intricately shaped glass pieces than leaded projects, so their appearance is often more delicate in nature. Greater care must be taken when cutting and grinding the glass to assure a proper fit. In leaded projects, came overlaps the glass in the channel, disguising places that aren't cut or ground precisely. If two glass pieces in a foiled panel don't fit well, their gaps have to be filled with solder, leaving an uneven seam. Making templates for copper foil projects promotes accuracy, conserves glass, and enhances the projects's final appearance.

Before applying copper foil, wash and dry the cut and smoothed glass piece to remove any dust. Peel away a small amount of backing paper from the end of the roll of copper foil. Center the copper foil tape on the edge of the glass piece and press down the middle of the tape. Continue to peel away more backing paper as you wrap the copper foil tape around the entire piece of glass (photo 22). Overlap ¼-inch (6 mm) of copper foil tape past your starting point, and cut off the excess tape with scissors. Fold down the corners of the copper foil tape and adhere them to the glass piece (photo 23). Press down the tape along the sides of the glass piece. If using a foil crimper, squeeze and pull

Photo 22

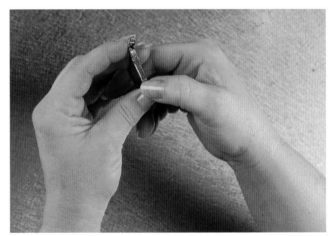

Photo 23

Photo 24

around the edges of the glass piece to seal the foil (photo 24). If using a burnisher, lay the glass piece down on your work surface, and rub all the sides and ends of the foiled glass to achieve a good seal.

Note: If the project is framed with a U-channel came, the outside edges of the perimeter glass pieces don't need to be foiled. Overlap the corner of the glass piece with ¼ inch (6 mm) of copper foil tape on each end.

TACK SOLDERING

Once all foiled glass pieces are in position, you don't want to risk any movement during soldering. Flux all key areas, such as where two or more pieces meet. Melt a small amount of solder—just enough to hold everything in place—and apply it at these points. These bumps of solder will be smoothed out later when you're soldering the seams.

TINNING OR FLAT-FILL SOLDERING

Tinning or flat-fill soldering is the next step in building a strong copper foil panel. Once the joints are tack soldered, flux all foiled-glass seams. Hold your solder wire above the tacked joint, melt the solder with the iron, and run a thin layer of solder along the foiled seam (photo 25).

HIGH-BEAD SOLDERING

Bead soldering puts the finishing touches on the foiled seams. Flux the intersection of two soldered seams, then use your iron to deposit a smooth rounded bead of solder at this point. Flux an adjoining seam and, with a steady hand, move the tip of the soldering iron very slowly down the tinned or flat-filled seam (photo 26). Work slowly and with care to create a smoother and more rounded seam.

Photo 25

Photo 26

PERSONAL SAFETY AND TOOL MAINTENANCE

Crafting stained glass isn't dangerous as long as you keep basic safety precautions in mind. The edges of cut glass are sharp and can cut you if carelessly handled. Keep your mind on your work whenever you're handling glass. This is also true for the wheel on the glass cutter. Have basic first aid supplies nearby, in case of an accident. Whenever you break glass, tiny particles will land on your work surface and the surrounding area. Make sure these places can be cleaned with a sponge or mop. You may want to wear a dust mask, goggles,

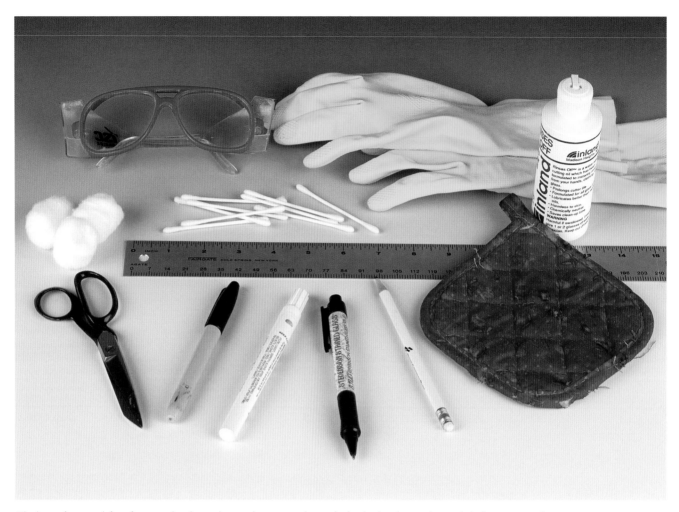

Clockwise from top left: safety goggles, latex gloves, glass cutter oil, metal ruler, kitchen hot pad, pencil, ballpoint pen, white paint pen, permanent marker, scissors, cotton swabs, cotton-tipped swabs

and rubber gloves when working with lead and other chemicals such as flux and patina. Whenever you handle solder or lead, keep your hands away from food, pets, and your face until your hands are properly cleaned. Also, wash your hands before and after proceeding to another activity. Lead is only dangerous when ingested.

Always read the manufacturer's instructions that come with your tools and supplies. The tips of new soldering irons, for example, may need to be tinned (coated with solder) before they're used. Store your stained glass tools in a clean box in a dry area to prevent rust. Dry your glass grinder thoroughly when it's not in use. Keep flux off your tools and skin as it's corrosive. Keep flux brushes in a jar so that flux from their tips doesn't harm other tools. Finally, glass tools are expressly designed for working with glass. It's inappropriate to use them for other craft or household projects.

Basic Stained Glass Tool Kit

Glass cutter

Glass cutter oil

Breaking pliers

Grozing pliers

Hacksaw

Lead nippers

Hammer

Horseshoe nails

Lead and zinc bumpers

Wire brush

Liquid or paste flux

Flux brush

Flux remover (for liquid flux) or acetone (for paste flux)

Soldering iron, 900° F (500° C) for lead or 1000° (537° C) for copper foil

Soldering iron stand

Solid core solder, 50/50 for lead or 60/40 for copper foil

Permanent marker

Glass cleaner

Paper towels or lint-free cloth

For copper foil projects add:

Pattern shears

Scissors

Poster board, or heavyweight paper

Carbon paper

Ruler

Glass grinder, or carbide stone

Foil crimper or burnisher

Bevy of Bevels Panel

Designer
CHRISTINE
KELLMANN
STEVENSON

BEVELED EDGES,
CUT AND POLISHED
TO REFLECT LIGHT,
ARE THE FOCAL
POINT OF THIS
CONTEMPORARY
CREATION. CLEAR
GLASS IS POSITIVELY
COMPELLING ON
ITS OWN WITHOUT
THE ALLURE OF
COLOR. THIS IS A
FINE PROJECT THAT
CONCENTRATES ON
DEVELOPING YOUR
LEADING SKILLS.

What You Do

1 Place the photocopied template on your work surface with the design facing up. Put the piece of clear hammered stained glass on top of the template, making sure the smooth side of the glass faces up. Use the permanent marker to trace the shape of and number pattern pieces 2, 3, 7, and 8.

2 Cut out the pieces of hammered glass on the inside edge of the marked lines. You may need to fit each piece of cut glass to the template by grozing, then grinding or sanding.

3 Use the hacksaw to cut a length of the U-channel zinc came longer than the width of the bottom line of the template. With the hammer and horseshoe nails, secure the zinc strip in place near the bottom of your work surface.

4 Slide Glass Piece 1 into place on the template, making sure it's in the channel of the zinc came. Attach lead bumpers to the other edges of Glass Piece 1 and secure them with horseshoe nails.

5 With the lead nippers, cut a piece of the H-channel lead came 36 inches (91.4 cm) long. Cut both ends so that each has a 90° angle. This length of lead came will be installed around the outer edges of Glass Pieces 2, 3, 7, and 8. You'll begin laying this piece of lead came at the top right corner of Glass Piece 1.

6 Position Glass Piece 2 on the template. Secure it in place by attaching lead bumpers to the top and right edges of the glass with horseshoe nails. Starting at the right corner, insert the lead came along the top edge of Glass Piece 1

What You Need

1 piece of hammered stained glass, 12 x 12 inches (30.5 x 30.5 cm), in clear

1 three-piece stained glass bevel cluster, in clear

2 stained glass bevels, 1 x 8 inches (2.5 x 20.3 cm), in clear

2 stained glass bevels, 1 x 6 inches (2.5 x 15.2 cm), in clear

4 stained glass corner bevels, 1 x 2 inches (2.5 x 5 cm), in clear

Basic stained glass tool kit (page 87)

Photocopy of design template (page 90) sized to 10 ¼ x 12 ¼ inches (25.6 x 30.6 cm)

¼-inch-wide (6 mm) U-channel zinc came

⁷⁄₃₂-inch-wide (5 mm) H-channel lead came

2 hanger loops of 18-gauge tinned wire

Needle-nose pliers

Hanging chain in the length and finish of your choice

Techniques You Need

Cutting Glass (page 80)

Grozing Glass (page 75)

Soldering (page 83)

(bottom of Glass Piece 2), pulling out the horseshoe nails and removing the bumpers as you go. Install the lead came up along the left edge of Glass Piece 2. Lock the lead came in place on the left edge of Glass Piece 2 with horseshoe nails. Now glass pieces 1 and 2 are secure.

7 With the tile nippers, cut a piece of lead came 4 inches (10.2 cm) long to go between Glass Pieces 1 and 3. Replace the bumper holding the lower right edge of Glass Piece 2 with this new piece of lead came. Add Glass Piece 3 onto the pattern, sliding it into the top came of Glass Piece 1 and the new 4-inch (10.2 cm) piece of came. Attach lead bumpers to all other edges of Glass Piece 3 with horseshoe nails.

8 Following the template and using the same method of cutting and applying lead came, proceed to add Glass Pieces 4, 5, and 6. Where two sections of lead came meet, cut their edges at corresponding angles so they'll fit together rather than overlap.

9 Install Glass Pieces 7 and 8. Curve the long length of lead came that you cut in step 5 all the way around Glass Pieces 7, 8, and 3, and back to where it started. Hammer horseshoe nails into your work surface to hold the lead in place as you go. All the interior glass pieces are now leaded.

10 Cut small pieces of lead came with the lead nippers to fit between the glass sections that form the panel's outside border. These pieces, eight in all (two near each corner), join the interior lead came edge with the zinc frame. Insert Glass Pieces 9, 10, 11, 12, 13, 14, and 15 one at a time into the lead came. Place zinc bumpers against all outer edges of the glass using horseshoe nails to hold them in place.

11 Use the hacksaw to cut strips of U-channel zinc came for the remaining three sides of the frame. Replace the zinc bumpers with these longer lengths of came, mitering the corners.

12 Heat the soldering iron. Use the needle-nose pliers to insert one hanger loop into the top of a side piece of zinc came. Rub the loop on both sides with the wire brush, then flux and solder the loop in place. Once cooled, test the solder joint by grabbing and tugging the loop with the needle-nose pliers. If the hanger comes off, resolder. Repeat this process to add the second hanger loop.

13 Brush all the lead and zinc came joints with the wire brush. Flux and solder each joint. Clean the flux residue off the soldered joints

14 Carefully turn over the panel, and repeat step 13.

15 Buff all soldered joints to a shine with a cloth or paper towel. Remove all stray marks or numbers with the glass cleaner. With needle-nose pliers, attach one side of the hanging chain to each hanger loop.

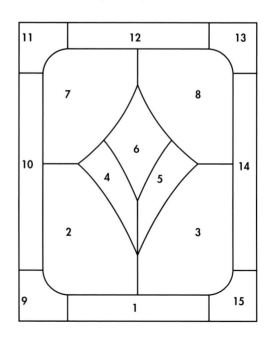

Tulip Bravado

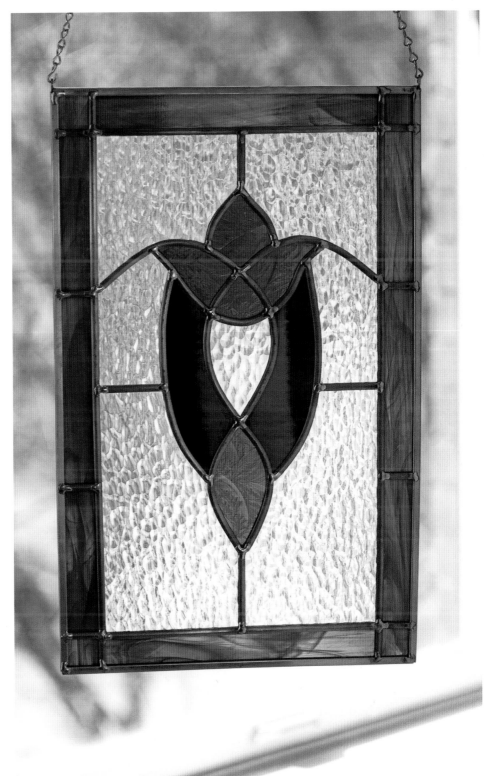

Designer
CHRISTINE
KELLMANN
STEVENSON

A FRESH INTERPRETATION
OF A CLASSIC DESIGN,
THIS DELIGHTFUL TULIP
PANEL BRINGS SPRING
INDOORS ALL YEAR
ROUND. OPAQUE
GLASSES IN SHADES OF
WINE UNITE TO FORM A
DISTINCTIVE AND
SOPHISTICATED PANEL.

What You Need

1 piece of glue-chip stained glass, 6 x 6 inches (15.2 cm x 15.2 cm), in medium wine

1 piece of stained water-glass, 6 x 6 inches (15.2 cm x 15.2 cm), in dark wine

1 piece of hammered stained glass, 6 x 6 inches (15.2 cm x 15.2 cm), in clear

1 piece of wispy stained glass, 12 x 12 inches (30.5 x 30.5 cm), in medium wine

Basic stained glass supply kit (page 87)

Photocopy of design template (page 93) sized to 10 ½ x 16 ½ inches (26.7 x 41.9 cm)

¼-inch-wide (6 mm) U-channel zinc came

7/32-inch-wide (5 mm) H-channel lead came

2 hanger loops of 18-gauge tinned wire

Needle-nose pliers

Hanging chain in the length and finish of your choice

Techniques You Need

Cutting Glass (page 80)

Grozing Glass (page 75)

Soldering (page 83)

What You Do

1 Place the photocopied template on your work surface with the design facing up. Use the permanent marker to trace the shapes of the pattern pieces onto the stained glasses. Number each pattern piece on the surface of the glass as you trace the shape.

2 Cut out the pieces of stained glass on the inside edge of the marked lines. You may need to fit each piece of cut glass to the template by grozing, then grinding or sanding.

3 To assemble this project, start at the top and work down. Use the hacksaw to cut a length of the U-channel zinc came longer than the width of the top line of the template. With the hammer and horseshoe nails, secure the zinc strip in place vertically on the right side of your work surface.

4 Slide Glass Piece 1 into place on the template, making sure that it's in the channel of the zinc came frame. Attach lead bumpers to the other edges of Glass Piece 1 and secure them in place with horseshoe nails.

5 Measure the length of lead came needed to run along the left edge (as seen on your work surface) of Glass Piece 1. With the lead nippers, cut a piece of lead came a little longer than this measurement. Remove the horseshoe nails and lead bumpers from the left edge of Glass Piece 1. Feed the cut lead came onto Glass Piece 1, making sure the glass is fully inserted into the channel. Hammer horseshoe nails around the edges of the lead came to hold it in place.

6 Position Glass Piece 2 on the template. Repeat steps 4 and 5 to install Glass Piece 2 and all remaining pieces of cut glass in numerical order. All the interior pieces are now leaded.

7 Use the hacksaw to cut strips of U-channel zinc came for the remaining three sides of the frame. Replace the zinc bumpers with these longer lengths of came, mitering the corners.

8 Heat the soldering iron. Use the needle-nose pliers to insert one hanger loop into the top of a side piece of zinc came. Rub the loop on both sides with the wire brush. Flux and solder the loop solidly in place. Repeat this process to add the second loop.

9 Brush all the lead and zinc came joints with the wire brush. Flux and solder each joint. Clean the flux residue off the soldered joints.

10 Carefully turn over the panel, and repeat step 9.

11 Buff all soldered joints to a shine with a cloth or paper towel. Remove all stray marks or numbers with the glass cleaner. With needle-nose pliers, attach one side of the hanging chain to each hanger loop.

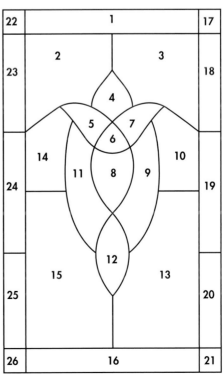

Mountain Twilight

Designer

CHRISTINE KELLMANN STEVENSON

THIS EXPRESSIVE PANEL USES SWIRLING, IRIDESCENT STAINED GLASSES TO DEPICT THE BRILLIANT COLORS OF

A SETTING SUN. THE MOUNTAINS' GENTLE SLOPES PROVIDE GREAT PRACTICE CUTTING CURVED GLASS.

HANG IT IN ANY WINDOW AND ALWAYS HAVE A ROOM WITH A VIEW!

What You Do

1 Place the photocopied template on your work surface with the design facing up. Use the permanent marker to trace the shapes of the pattern pieces onto the stained glasses. Number each pattern piece on the surface of the glass.

2 Cut out the pieces of stained glass on the inside edge of the marked lines. You may need to fit each piece of cut glass to the template by grozing, then grinding or sanding.

3 Use the hacksaw to cut a length of the U-channel zinc came longer than the width of the bottom line of the template. With the hammer and horseshoe nails, secure the zinc strip in place near the bottom of your work surface.

4 Slide Glass Piece 1 into place on the template, making sure it's in the channel of the zinc came. Attach lead bumpers to the other edges of Glass Piece 1 and secure them in place with horseshoe nails.

5 Measure the length of lead came needed to run along the top edge of Glass Piece 1. Using the lead nippers, cut a piece of lead came a little longer than this measurement. Remove the horseshoe nails and bumpers from the top edge of Glass Piece 1. Feed the cut lead came over Glass Piece 1, making sure the glass is fully inserted into the channel. Hammer horseshoe nails around the edges of the lead came to hold it in place.

6 With the tip of a horseshoe nail, scratch a mark on the lead came where it intersects with the lower strip of zinc frame. For a snug joint, use the lead nippers to cut, or miter, the lead came at this angle.

What You Need

1 piece of stained glass, 6 x 6 inches (15.2 x 15.2 cm), in each of these colors: gold, amber, blue, purple, green, and multi-colored opal

1 piece of stained glass, 18 x 18 inches (45.7 x 45. 7 cm), in each of these colors: pale purple, white, and iridized wispy

1 piece of stained glass, 12 x 12 inches (30.5 x 30.5 cm), in each of these colors: opal, purple, cobalt, and blue streaky

Basic stained glass tool kit (page 87)

Photocopy of design template (page 96) sized to 13 ½ x 8 inches (34.3 x 20.3 cm)

¼-inch-wide (6 mm) U-channel zinc came

7/32-inch-wide (5 mm) H-channel lead came

2 hanger loops of 18-gauge tinned wire

Needle-nose pliers

Hanging chain in the length and finish of your choice

Techniques You Need

Cutting Glass (page 80)

Grozing Glass (page 75)

Soldering (page 83)

7 Position Glass Piece 2 on the template. Repeat steps 4, 5, and 6 to install Glass Piece 2 and all remaining pieces of cut glass in numerical order. All the interior pieces are now leaded.

8 Use the hacksaw to cut strips of U-channel zinc came for the remaining three sides of the frame. Replace the zinc bumpers with these longer lengths of came, mitering the corners.

9 Heat the soldering iron. Use the needle-nose pliers to insert one hanger loop into the top of a side piece of zinc came. Rub the loop on both sides with the wire brush. Flux and solder the loop solidly in place. Repeat this process to add the second hanger loop.

10 Brush all the lead and zinc came joints with the wire brush. Flux and solder each joint. Clean the flux residue off the soldered joints.

11 Carefully turn over the panel, and repeat step 10.

12 Buff all soldered joints to a shine with a cloth or paper towel. Remove all stray marks or numbers with the glass cleaner. With needle-nose pliers, attach one side of the hanging chain to each hanger loop.

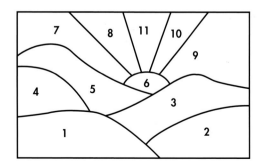

Mighty Tree Lamp

Designer

CHRISTINE KELLMANN STEVENSON

THE TIMELESS IMAGE OF A MATURE TREE MAKES A HANDSOME STAINED GLASS LAMP SHADE. THE NATURAL CONTOUR OF THE TREETOP IS REINFORCED BY HIGH-BEAD SOLDERING INSTEAD OF A FRAME. ILLUMINATE YOUR WORLD BY GETTING BACK TO NATURE.

What You Need

1 piece of stained glass, 6 x 6 inches (15.2 x 15.2 cm), in water-glass (olive on sea-green), amber, and black

1 piece of stained glass, 12 x 12 inches (30.5 x 30.5 cm), in grey water-glass

Basic stained glass tool kit (page 87)

Photocopy of design template (page 99)

7/32-inch-wide (5 mm) copper foil tape, black-backed*

Black patina for solder

Cotton-tipped swabs

Kitchen hot pad

Wood lamp base with electrical cord and socket (the base of the tree must fit into a slot in the lamp base)

The black-backed foil blends well with the light grey water-glass and black solder seam.

Techniques You Need

Transferring an Image (page 79)

Using Pattern Shears (page 74)

Cutting Glass (page 80)

Grozing and Grinding Glass (pages 75, 82)

Applying Copper Foil Tape (page 84)

Tack Soldering (page 85)

Tinning or Flat-fill Soldering (page 85)

High-bead Soldering (page 85)

What You Do

1 Make a carbon paper transfer of the photocopied design onto heavyweight paper. Number all pattern pieces, and add directional arrows for the glass as needed. Cut around the perimeter of the pattern with regular scissors, then cut out the individual pattern pieces with the pattern shears.

2 Place one pattern piece on top of one stained glass piece. Trace the pattern piece's contour onto the glass with a permanent marker. Number the glass piece inside the lines, marking its direction with an arrow if needed. Be sure to mark the direction of the sky pieces. Repeat this process for each pattern piece on the appropriate glass.

3 Cut out each piece of stained glass on the inside of the marked lines. Groze and grind the edges of each piece to fit the pattern as precisely as possible.

4 Cover the edges of the glass pieces with copper foil tape.

5 Heat the soldering iron. Arrange all the foiled pieces of glass on top of the template and make sure the project is level and square. Lightly flux and tack solder all joints on the outer perimeter.

6 Flux the length of every foiled seam. Flat-fill solder every seam except where the perimeter glass pieces will be inserted into the zinc came frame.

7 High-bead solder on top of the flat-filled seams. Clean the flux residue off the soldered joints.

8   Carefully turn over the panel. Some of the solder from the front side of the panel may have come through the seams. Repeat steps 5, 6, and 7 for the back side of the panel.

9   Using the kitchen hot pad, hold the project over your work surface with the base of the tree up in the air. Lightly high-bead solder the tree's bottom edge. As it solidifies turn the project a little more, continuing to high-bead solder the outer edge. This extra solder gives the copper foil tape enough strength to hold the piece together. Hold the project over the board at all times and take care not to drip any solder on your hands or arms while high-beading in the air.

10   Clean the stained glass thoroughly. Read and follow the manufacturer's instructions and safety precautions on the bottle of black patina. Pour a small amount of the black patina into its bottle cap. Dip a cotton-tipped swab into the solution and wipe it onto the panel's solder lines. Try not to get the patina on the surface of the glass. Remove the black patina from the solder lines by wiping them with a clean cotton-tipped swab. Repeat this process until you're satisfied with the black finish. Clean any patina off the glass surface immediately.

11   Remove all stray marks or numbers from the stained glass with the glass cleaner. Insert the stained glass panel into the lamp base, and install a night-light bulb into its socket.

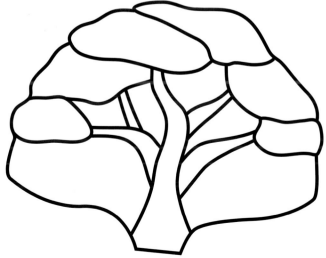

Victorian Crimson Crown

Designer
CHRISTINE KELLMANN STEVENSON

REMINISCENT OF ROYAL FINERY, THIS STAINED GLASS PANEL HAS A SPARKLING MIX OF COLOR, TEXTURE, AND DIMENSION. USING SUBTLE-COLORED BACKGROUND GLASSES INCREASES THE INTENSITY OF THE CENTRAL RED MOTIF. WITH THIS VERSATILE DESIGN YOU CAN PICK ANY GLASS FOR THE INNER CROWN TO FIT YOUR DECOR.

What You Do

1 Make a carbon paper transfer of the photo-copied design onto heavyweight paper. Number all pattern pieces, and add directional arrows for the glass as needed. Cut around the perimeter of the pattern with regular scissors, then cut out the individual pattern pieces with the pattern shears. Pattern pieces aren't required for the precut stained glass bevels.

2 Place one pattern piece on top of one stained glass piece. Trace the pattern piece's contour onto the glass with a permanent marker. Number the glass piece inside the lines, marking its direction with an arrow if needed. Repeat this process for each pattern piece on the appropriate glass.

3 Cut out each piece of stained glass on the inside of the marked lines. Groze and grind the edges of each piece to fit the pattern as precisely as possible.

4 Cover the edges of the glass pieces with copper foil tape.

5 Heat the soldering iron. Arrange all the foiled pieces of glass on top of the template and make sure the project is level and square. Flux and tack solder all joints on the outer perimeter.

6 Flux the length of every foiled seam. Solder every seam except where the perimeter glass pieces will be inserted into the channel of the zinc came. Flat-fill the seams with solder and cover all the copper foil tape.

7 High-bead solder on top of the flat-filled seams. Clean the flux residue off the soldered joints.

What You Need

6 stained glass bevels, 1 x 1 inch (2.5 x 2.5 cm), in clear

1 piece of stained glass, 12 x 12 inches (30.5 x 30.5 cm), in apricot peach

1 piece of stained glass, 6 x 6 inches (15.2 x 15.2 cm), in red

Basic stained glass tool kit (page 87)

Photocopy of design template (page 102) sized to 8 x 10 3/8 inches (20.3 x 26.4 cm)

1/4-inch-wide (6 mm) U-channel zinc came

7/32-inch-wide (5 mm) copper foil tape

2 hanger loops of 18-gauge tinned wire

Needle-nose pliers

Hanging chain in the length and finish of your choice

Techniques You Need

Transferring an Image (page 79)
Using Pattern Shears (page 74)
Cutting Glass (page 80)
Grozing and Grinding Glass (pages 75, 82)
Applying Copper Foil Tape (page 84)
Tack Soldering (page 85)
Tinning or Flat-fill Soldering (page 85)
High-bead Soldering (page 85)

8 Carefully turn over the panel. Some of the solder from the front side of the panel may have come through the seams. Repeat steps 5, 6, and 7 on the back side of the panel.

9 Turn over the panel and lay it down on your work surface. With the hacksaw, cut a length of stretched zinc came to fit each edge of the frame. Remember that the length of the came needs to extend past the panel in order for the frame joints to be mitered. Fit the soldered stained glass panel into the U-channel of the zinc came. Hammer horseshoe nails around the edges of the frame.

10 Use the needle-nose pliers to insert one hanger loop into the top of a side piece of zinc came. Rub the loop on both sides with the wire brush. Flux and solder the loop solidly in place. Repeat this process to add the second hanger loop.

11 Wire brush the zinc came at the frame corners and every place it touches soldered seams. Flux and lightly solder all corners and connecting seams. Clean the flux residue off the soldered joints. Buff all soldered joints to a shine with a cloth or paper towel.

12 Remove the horseshoe nails, turn over the panel, and repeat step 11.

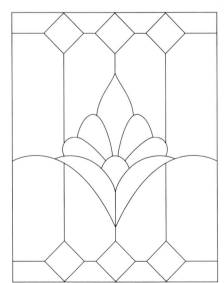

Panda Appeal

DESIGNER
CHRISTINE
KELLMANN
STEVENSON

THE PANDA'S CHARM IS UNIVERSAL, AND THE DIGNITY OF THIS COMPOSITION SUITS OUR BLACK AND WHITE FRIEND. THE LARGE PANEL PIECES LET YOU GET THE MOST OUT OF FANTASTIC STAINED GLASSES. THE DELICATE EYES, NOSE, AND LEAVES ARE DETAILS EXCLUSIVE TO THE COPPER FOIL METHOD.

What You Need

1 piece of stained glass, 6 x 6 inches (15.2 x 15.2 cm), in each of these colors: lamp beige, black water-glass, dark green, white, and gold-pink opal

1 piece of stained glass, 24 x 24 inches (61 x 61 cm), in white wispy

Basic stained glass tool kit (page 87)

Photocopy of design template (page 105) sized to 10¼ x 16 inches (26 x 40.6 cm)

¼-inch-wide (6 mm) U-channel zinc came

7/32-inch-wide (5 mm) copper foil tape

2 hanger loops of 18-gauge tinned wire

Copper patina for solder

Copper patina for zinc

Cotton-tipped swabs

Steel wool

Hanging chain in the length and finish of your choice

Note: The center of the panda's nose is too small to cut, foil, and install a glass piece. Leave an open gap in the design until the end of the project, then fill it with solder. The two small bamboo leaves at the panda's mouth are cut freehand instead of from a pattern. After sanding and foiling their edges, place the leaves aside. They're soldered onto the surface of the finished panel for a three-dimensional effect.

Techniques You Need

What You Do

1 Make a carbon paper transfer of the photo-copied design onto heavyweight paper. Number all pattern pieces, and add directional arrows for the glass as needed. Cut around the perimeter of the pattern with regular scissors, then cut out the individual pattern pieces with the pattern shears.

2 Place one pattern piece on top of one stained glass piece. Trace the pattern piece's contour onto the glass with a permanent marker. Number the glass piece inside the lines, marking its direction with an arrow if needed. Repeat this process for each pattern piece on the appropriate glass.

3 Cut out each piece of stained glass on the inside of the marked lines. Groze and grind the edges of each piece to fit the pattern precisely as possible.

4 Cover the edges of the glass pieces with copper foil tape.

5 Heat the soldering iron. Arrange all the foiled pieces of glass on top of the template, making sure the project is level and square. Lightly flux and tack solder all joints on the outer perimeter.

6 Flux the length of every foiled seam. Flat-fill solder every seam except where the perimeter glass pieces will be inserted into the channel of the zinc came.

7 High-bead solder on top of the flat-filled seams. Clean the flux residue off the soldered joints.

8 Carefully turn the panel over. Some of the solder from the front side of the panel may have come through the seams. Repeat steps 5, 6, and 7 on the back side of the panel.

9 Turn the panel over and lay it down on your work surface with the front side facing up. With the hacksaw, cut a length of stretched zinc came to fit each edge of the frame. Remember that the length of the came needs to extend past the panel in order for the frame joints to be mitered. Fit the soldered panel into the U-channel of the zinc came frame. Hammer horseshoe nails around the edges of the frame to hold them in place.

10 Use the needle-nose pliers to insert one hanger loop into the top of a side piece of zinc came. Rub the loop on both sides with the wire brush. Flux and solder the loop solidly in place. Repeat this process to add the second hanger loop.

11 Wire brush the zinc came at the frame corners and every place it touches sol-

dered seams. Flux and lightly solder all corners and connecting seams. Clean the flux residue off the soldered joints. Buff all soldered joints to a shine with a cloth or paper towel.

12 Turn over the panel and lay it down on your work surface. Repeat step 11 on the back side of the panel.

13 Flux the cut, sanded, and foiled bamboo leaves. Lightly solder one leaf to the second leaf. Clean the flux from the leaves. Needle-nose pliers are helpful when working with small pieces.

14 Read and follow the manufacturer's instructions and safety precautions on the bottle of copper patina. Pour a small amount of the copper patina into its bottle cap. Dip a cotton-tipped swab into the solution and wipe it onto the panel's solder lines. Try not to get the patina on the surface of the glass. Remove the copper patina from the solder lines by wiping them with a clean cotton-tipped swab. Repeat this process until you're satisfied with the copper finish. Clean any patina off the glass surface immediately. Repeat this step to patina the two bamboo leaves.

15 Rub the zinc came with the steel wool, then clean the frame. Follow the same application instructions found in step 14 using the copper patina for zinc.

16 Turn over the panel and repeat steps 14 and 15 for the back side of the panel.

17 Heat the soldering iron. Flux the solder near the panda's mouth, then flux the bamboo leaves. Position the bamboo leaves on the panel and hold them in place with a cotton-tipped

swab. Lightly solder the leaves in the desired location. Clean off any flux residue, and reapply the copper patina if necessary.

18 Remove all stray marks or numbers from the stained glass with the glass cleaner. Attach one side of the hanging chain to each hanger loop using the needle-nose pliers.

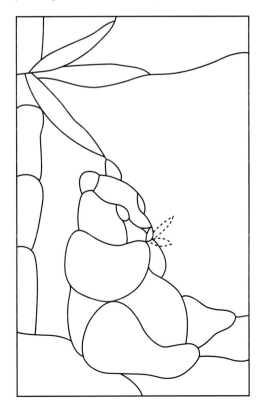

Perfectly Poised Pastel Mobile

Designer
JENNIFER E. MITCHELL

BALANCE IS AT THE HEART OF
ALL MOBILES, BUT THIS ONE
OUTSHINES THE REST BY
EMBRACING THE BEAUTY OF
STAINED GLASS. PLUS, THE
COLOR, FORM, AND SIZE OF
THE INDIVIDUAL ELEMENTS
CREATE HARMONY AND CAST
GORGEOUS PASTEL SHADOWS.
SILVER-BACKED FOIL ADDS
EXTRA BRIGHTNESS.

What You Do

MAKING THE SMALL CIRCLE ORNAMENT

1 Measure and mark a half-circle with a 2-inch (5 cm) diameter on the heavyweight paper using the permanent marker. Cut out the half-circle pattern with scissors. Place this pattern on top of a piece of stained glass and trace around the shape with the permanent marker. Place the same pattern on top of a different-colored piece of stained glass and trace around the shape.

2 Cut out each half-circle of stained glass on the inside of the marked lines. Groze and grind the edges of each piece to precisely fit their measurements. Compare the cut glass pieces to each other. Mark any protruding edges with the permanent marker, then grind them off.

3 Foil both half-circle glass pieces.

4 Heat the soldering iron. Place both foiled half-circles on your work surface with their straight sides connecting to form a level circle. Flux the center seam of the circle. Tack solder the two outer points of the seam. Flat fill the seam with solder. Turn over the ornament, flux, then tack and flat-fill solder the center seam. Flux and tin the edge of the circle. High-bead solder the seam and edge.

5 Place the small circle ornament into the vise clamp with the center seam vertical. Flux one jewelry hoop at the top point of the circle at its vertical seam. Using the needle-nose pliers to grip the jewelry hoop, solder it to the small circle. Clean the flux off the small circle.

What You Need

Stained glass in assorted pastel colors

2 stained glass bevels, 1 x 3 inches (2.5 x 7.6 cm), in clear

Basic stained glass tool kit (page 87)

7/32-inch (5 mm) copper foil tape, silver-backed

Vise clamp attached to table

Needle-nose pliers

1 brass rod, 1/8 x 36 inches (3 mm x 91 cm)

Transparent nylon line, 12 to 14 lb (5.5 to 6.4 kg) test

1/4-inch-wide (6 mm) jewelry hoops, approximately 20

14-gauge steel wire, approximately 10 inches (25.4 cm)

Metal file

Finishing compound

Polishing cloth

Techniques You Need

Cutting Glass (page 80)

Grozing and Grinding Glass (pages 75, 82)

Applying Copper Foil Tape (page 84)

Tack Soldering (page 85)

Tinning or Flat-fill soldering (page 85)

High-bead Soldering (page 85)

MAKING THE LARGE CIRCLE ORNAMENT

1 Measure and mark a half-circle with a 3-inch (7.6 cm) diameter on the heavyweight paper. Cut out the half-circle pattern with scissors. Use the permanent marker to trace around the pattern on top of three different colors of stained glass. Draw a straight line across the glass to form quarter-circles on two of the half-circles.

2 Cut out each piece of stained glass on the inside of the marked lines. After cutting the glass you'll have one half-circle in one color, two quarter-circles in a second color, and two quarter-circles in a third color.

3 Groze and grind the edges of the half-circle and two quarter-circles of different-colored glasses. When joined, these three pieces form a circle with a 3-inch (7.6 cm) diameter.

4 Foil the half-circle and the two quarter-circles of stained glass.

5 Heat the soldering iron. Arrange the three foiled pieces into a full circle. The seams should be touching and level. Flux the seams, then tack solder the three outer points on the seams to hold the circle in place. Flat fill the seams with solder. Turn over the ornament, flux, then tack and flat-fill solder the seams. Flux and tin the edges of the circle. High-bead solder the seams and edge.

6 Attach a jewelry hoop to the top of the large circle ornament following the technique described in step 5 of Making the Small Circle Ornament.

MAKING THE RECTANGLE ORNAMENT

1 Measure and mark one 1 x 3-inch (2.5 x 7.6 cm) rectangle, one 1 x 2-inch (2.5 x 5 cm) rectangle, and one 1 x 1-inch (2.5 x 2.5 cm) square on the heavyweight paper. Cut out the patterns with scissors. Place these three pattern pieces on top of three different-colored pieces of stained glass and trace around the shapes with the permanent marker.

2 Cut out each piece of stained glass on the inside of the marked lines. Groze and grind the edges. Lay the cut glass pieces flush against one another and check their combined measurement. When joined, these three pieces form a 2 x 3-inch (5 x 7.6 cm) rectangle.

3 Foil the edges of the three stained glass pieces.

4 Heat the soldering iron. Place the 1 x 3-inch (2.5 x 7.6 cm) rectangle flat on your work surface in a vertical position. Place the 1 x 1-inch (2.5 x 2.5 cm) square glass piece to the right of the large rectangle. Adjust the two pieces so they're even at the top. Place the 1 x 2-inch (2.5 x 5 cm) small rectangle directly beneath the square. All three glass pieces should be touching, level, and square. Flux the seams where the stained glass pieces meet. Tack solder the three outer points and the interior point where three corners meet. Flat fill the seams with solder. Turn over the ornament, flux, then tack and flat-fill solder the seams. Flux and tin the edges of the rectangle. High-bead solder the seams and edges.

5 Attach a jewelry hoop in the center of the top of the rectangle ornament, as described in step 5 of Making the Small Circle Ornament.

MAKING THE TURNED CIRCLES ORNAMENT

1 Measure and mark one circle with a 1½-inch (3.8 cm) diameter and one circle with a 1¼-inch (3.2 cm) diameter on the heavyweight paper. Cut out the patterns with scissors. Place these pattern pieces on top of two different colors of stained glass and trace around their shapes with the permanent marker. Trace the circle with the 1¼-inch (3.2 cm) diameter again on a third color of stained glass. You'll have a total of three circles outlined on three colors of glass.

2 Cut out each piece of stained glass on the inside of the marked lines. Groze and grind the edges of each piece to precisely fit their measurement.

3 Foil the edges of all three stained glass circles.

4 Heat the soldering iron. Flux the edges of all foiled circles. Tin the foil tape on the edge of each circle.

5 Secure the circle with the 1½-inch (3.8 cm) diameter in the vise clamp. Hold one small circle on top of the large circle. Rotate the small circle so its glass face is perpendicular to the glass face of the large circle. Flux the point where the circles meet on both edges of solder. Tack solder the two circles together. Remove the glass from the vise clamp, and make sure the circles are evenly attached. Completely solder the joint together.

6 Re-secure the ornament in the vise clamp with the larger circle on top. Repeat step 5 to attach the second small circle.

7 Attach a jewelry hoop in the center of the top of the turned circles ornament, as described in step 5 of Making the Small Circle Ornament.

MAKING THE CIRCLE AND DIAMOND ORNAMENT

1 Measure and mark one circle with a 1¼-inch (3.2 cm) diameter and one 1¼ x 1¼-inch (3.2 x 3.2 cm) square on the heavyweight paper. Cut out the patterns with scissors. Place the patterns on top of two different-colored pieces of stained glass and trace around the shapes with the permanent marker.

2 Cut out the circle and the square from the stained glass. Groze and grind the edges smooth.

3 Foil the edges of the circle and the square.

4 Heat the soldering iron. Flux and lightly solder the edges of the foiled circle and the foiled square.

5 Use the wire cutters to cut a piece of the 14-gauge steel wire that's approximately 4 to 5 inches (10.2 to 12.7 cm) long. Twist and loop the wire by hand to create an interesting design. Trim the ends of the wire to the length you desire with the wire cutters. Flux and apply a small amount of solder to each end of the wire.

6 Place the square into the vise clamp with one corner pointing straight up to form a diamond shape. Flux the top point of the diamond, and attach one end of the twisted wire with solder. Remove the piece from the vise clamp to make sure the wire is vertical and lines up with the points of the diamond.

7 Secure the circle in the vice clamp. Flux the top point of the circle and attach the free end of the twisted wire with solder. The glass face of the circle should be perpendicular to the glass face of the diamond. Remove the ornament from the vice clamp and ensure that all the elements line up nicely.

8 Attach a jewelry hoop in the center of the top of the circle, as described in step 5 of Making the Small Circle Ornament.

MAKING THE BOX ORNAMENT

1 Measure and mark one 1 x 2-inch (2.5 x 5 cm) rectangle and one 1 x 1-inch (2.5 x 2.5 cm) square on the heavyweight paper. Cut out the patterns with scissors. Place each pattern on top of a different-colored piece of stained glass and trace around the shapes with the permanent marker. Place the two patterns on top of two more different-colored pieces of stained glass and trace each shape with the permanent marker.

2 Cut out the two rectangles and the two squares from the stained glass. Groze and grind the edges of each piece to precisely fit their measurement.

3 Foil the edges of the rectangles and the squares.

4 Foil the two precut 1 x 3-inch (2.5 x 7.6 cm) clear stained glass bevels. Flux and tin all foiled edges on both bevels.

5 Heat the soldering iron. Place one square glass piece on your work surface. Position one rectangular glass piece (not a bevel) directly above the square. The 1-inch (2.5 cm) widths of the glass pieces should be touching, level, and square. Flux the foiled seam between the two pieces of glass. Tack solder the two outer points on the seam. Flat-fill solder the seam. Repeat this process (flux, tack, then flat-fill solder) on the opposite side of the seam. High-bead solder both sides of the seam.

6 Repeat step 5 using the second cut and foiled square and rectangle.

7 Place one soldered bevel horizontally on its edge in the vise clamp. Place the horizontal edge of the rectangle created in step 5 on top of

MAKING THE BRASS HANGING RODS

1 Measure and mark four lengths on the ⅛ x 36-inch (3 mm x 91 cm) brass rod. The pieces of rod should measure 10 inches (25.4 cm), 5½ inches (14 cm), 5 inches (12.7 cm), and 4½ inches (11.4 cm). Secure the brass rod in the vise clamp, and cut the measured pieces with the hacksaw. Smooth all jagged ends with the metal file.

2 Heat the soldering iron. Flux and lightly solder the ends of all four rods. Flux and solder one ¼-inch (6 mm) jewelry hoop to each end of all four rods. Make sure the holes in the hoops face the same direction on both ends of the rod. The 10-inch (25.4 cm) rod requires a third jewelry hoop. Find the center point on the rod. Flux and solder a jewelry hoop to this point, making sure the new center-hoop faces the same direction as the end-hoops. Clean the flux off the rods.

the bevel's edge at a 90° angle. Flux the corner joints on both glass pieces and tack solder them together at each end.

8 Repeat step 7 using the second bevel and the rectangle created in step 6.

9 Join the two L-shaped pieces of glass to form a box that's 1 x 1 x 3 inches (2.5 x 2.5 x 7.6 cm), and open at the top and bottom. Flux and tack solder each corner joint.

10 Use the wire cutters to cut a 3-inch (7.6 cm) piece of the 14-gauge steel wire. Twist a small loop in the center of wire by hand. Trim off the ends of the wire with wire cutters so the loop fits diagonally across the open top of the box. Flux the ends of the wire and the corners of the box. Tack solder the hanging wire to the top of the box at diagonal corners. Clean any flux off the glass box ornament.

ATTACHING THE ORNAMENTS TO THE RODS AND BALANCING THE MOBILE

1 Cut two different lengths of nylon line. Attach the small circle ornament to one end of the 4½-inch (11.4 cm) brass rod using one piece of the cut nylon line. Feed the line through the jewelry hoop on the ornament and tie a secure knot. Feed the free end of the nylon line through the hoop on the rod and tie a secure knot. Attach the circle and diamond ornament to the opposite end of the 4½-inch (11.4 cm) rod using the same process.

2 Attach the rectangle and the turned circles ornaments to the 5-inch (12.7 cm) rod following the technique described in step 1.

3 To find the balance point of the two rods completed in steps 1 and 2, tie the end of a piece of nylon line to the middle of one rod. Move this nylon line side to side in small amounts until the rod balances. Mark this point on the rod with a pen. Repeat this step for the second rod.

4 Flux and lightly solder the marked balance points on both the 4½-inch (11.4 cm) and the 5-inch (12.7 cm) rods. Flux and solder one jewelry hoop to the balance point on each rod. Solder the hoop on the top edge, rather than the bottom edge, of the rod.

5 Cut two pieces of the nylon line. Tie the box ornament to one end-hoop of the 5½-inch (14 cm) brass rod with one piece of the nylon line. Tie one end of the second piece of nylon line to the balance hoop of the 4½-inch (11.4 cm) rod. Attach the second end of this nylon line to the empty end-hoop on the 5½-inch (14 cm) rod.

6 Find and mark the balance point of the brass rod completed in step 5 using the method described in step 3.

7 Flux and lightly solder the marked balance point on the 5½-inch (14 cm) rod. Flux one jewelry hoop and solder it to the balance point on the rod. Solder the jewelry hoop to the top edge, rather than the bottom edge, of the rod.

8 Cut a 4-inch (10.2 cm) piece of the nylon line. Feed one end of the nylon line through the hanging hoop on the large circle ornament and tie a secure knot. Feed the free end of the nylon line through the middle hanging hoop of the 10-inch (25.4 cm) rod. Adjust the line to the desired length of approximately 2 inches (5 cm) before securing it to the hoop on the rod.

9 Cut two long pieces of nylon line. Tie one end of the first piece of nylon line to the balance hoop on the 5½-inch (14 cm) rod and one end of the second piece of nylon line to the 5-inch (12.7 cm) rod. Attach the untied end of one line to one end-hoop of the 10-inch (25.4 cm) rod. Repeat this process for the second line and the second end-hoop on the 10-inch (25.4 cm) rod. Vary the lengths of both lines, making sure both rods hang below the large circle.

10 Find and mark the balance point of the 10-inch (25.4 cm) brass rod using the method described in step 3.

11 Flux and lightly solder the marked balance point on the 10-inch (25.4 cm) rod. Flux one jewelry hoop and solder it to the balance point of the rod. Solder the hoop to the top edge of the rod. This is the hanging hoop for the mobile.

12 Tie enough nylon line to the hanging hoop to create a satisfactory loop for hanging the mobile.

13 Clean all flux off the stained glass mobile. Apply the finishing compound to all ornaments, glass and solder, and to the brass rods. Let the compound dry, then polish with the polishing cloth.

Embellishment, Assembly, and Bottle Cutting

There are many ways to get crafty with glass. Embellishment, assembly, and bottle cutting are three dynamic and easy glass craft fields worthy of exploring.

Embellishment Materials and Techniques

A glass surface is a unique canvas on which you can collage many materials. Ordinary vases, bottles, and mirrors can be decorated with everything from tumbled glass shards to wrapping paper. This is an easy way to transform low-cost objects into one-of-a-kind gifts. It's also handy if you want to adapt glass to your own color scheme.

GLASS TO GLASS

ADHESIVES

Glass glues offer a permanent, clear, and waterproof bond. Although science has engineered a highly sophisticated range of glass adhesives, the embellishment projects in this book were all created with glues that you can buy in most craft supply or hardware stores. Clear epoxies are commonly used to bond glass to glass, while silicone adhesives are recommended for attaching other materials to glass. All glues and epoxies state on their labels whether or not they work with glass. As with all chemicals, closely follow the application procedures and safety precautions recommended by the manufacturer.

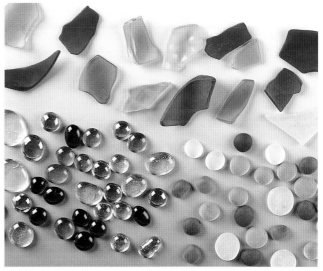

Standard and tumbled glass shards and half-marbles

HALF-MARBLES

Glass half-marbles are popular embellishments that come in many colors, shapes, and sizes. They range in clarity from transparent to opaque, and

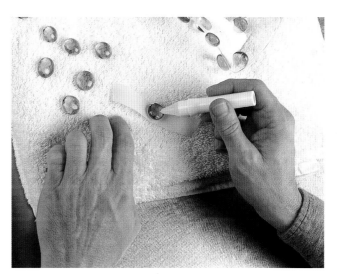

Photo 1

some even project an iridescent glow. Half-marbles have a smooth, level bottom that easily adheres to other flat glass surfaces with little effort. A dab of epoxy on the flat side of the marble will permanently join it to your project (photo 1). For increased stability during drying time, position a layer of masking tape over the marble to hold it in place (photo 2).

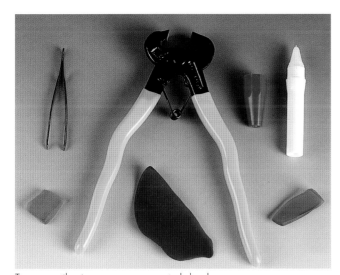

Tweezers, tile nippers, epoxy, assorted shards

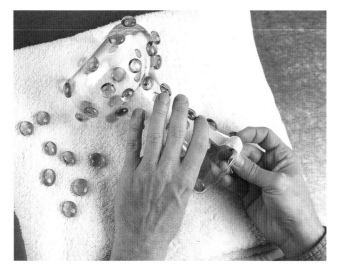

Photo 2

Photo 3

Half-marbles are delightful when combined with other glass craft techniques. Etching gives the Polka-Dot Vase on page 126 extra dimension, texture, and charm. Magnetic Personality on page 135 are half-marbles with reverse decoupage. The dome-shaped glass slightly distorts the images creating an interesting effect.

JEWELS

Anywhere a half-marble is used, a glass jewel can be substituted. With their beveled edges, glass jewels are fashioned to resemble precious stones. They deliver more complex patterns of reflected light than half-marbles. Both half-marbles and jewels can be tumbled at home to roughen their surfaces and produce a matte finish.

SHARDS

To make your own glass shards from bottles or jars, you'll need an old bath towel, newspaper, a hammer, safety goggles, and a sturdy pair of work gloves. Cover a strong, level work surface with newspapers. Fold the towel into a multilayered square and place it on top of the newspaper. Center your glass object between the layers of the

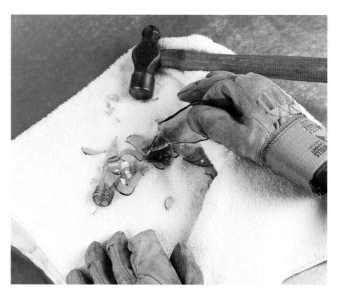

Photo 4

Photo 5

towel. Put on your safety goggles and gloves. With one hand, hold down the seams of the folded towel. Use the other hand to hammer the towel-wrapped glass object (photo 3). Lift back one corner of the towel to see the results (photo 4). If your shards are too large, repeat this process until you're satisfied with the result, or use tile nippers to trim any shard down to size (photo 5).

TUMBLED GLASS

With a texture similar to beach glass worn by the rolling ocean tides, tumbled glass is now commercially available in most craft stores. Look in the glass crafts department first, but you may also find pretumbled shards amongst the floral supplies. Tumbled glass is also be available wherever aquarium supplies are sold. If you can't find a specific color or shape, you're not out of luck. The high-gloss finish of any small glass surface, such as a marble, jewel, or bottle shard, can be worn away to a frosted finish simply and easily with a rock tumbler.

LAPIDARY TUMBLER

A lapidary (or rock) tumbler has a rotating barrel that simulates the action of waves. By using a more abrasive grit (silicon carbide) than sand and by maintaining a constant speed of rotation, tumblers produce artificial beach glass in a fraction of the natural time. Shards of glass placed in the tumbler are continually cascaded down its walls and through a coarse abrasive slurry. The desired matte finish and rounded blunt shape is achieved after six to eight hours, a short time in the lapidary world. Only a hobby-quality rock tumbler is needed to work with glass, although more expensive varieties are available.

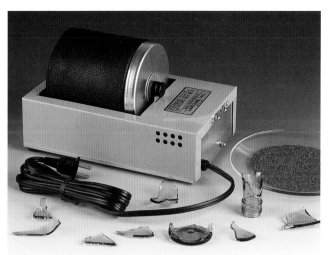

Lapidary tumbler, silicon carbide grit, glass shards

DECOUPAGE

Are you attracted to the patterns you see printed in magazines or on paper products? Have you ever made a collage of meaningful images or keepsake memorabilia? Even if you haven't thought of expressing yourself creatively through paper assemblage, you'll soon find decoupage to be a simple and rewarding craft. Decoupage is the art of decorating a surface with paper cutouts. This straightforward embellishment technique can be applied to glassware with marvelous results, transforming everyday objects into one-of-a-kind works of art. The few art supplies you'll need are inexpensive and widely available.

CUTTING TOOLS

A pair of good scissors with sharp blades is a great asset for decoupage. It's even better, but by no means necessary, to have a few different types of scissors. Standard-size utility scissors, small-bladed sewing scissors, and scissors with a curved-blade would certainly handle all of your cutting needs. A fixed-blade craft knife also helps when cutting precise lines against a straightedge or scoring around a template. Change your knife blade often, because a dull, dirty, or damaged blade causes ragged edges on paper cutouts.

Decoupage supplies, including clear aerosol varnish and decoupage medium

PAINTBRUSHES

Since you'll be applying the decoupage medium to the glass with a paintbrush, you'll want to have a small selection at your disposal. The size of the paintbrush should correspond to the size of the paper cutouts to be decoupaged. Use a brush with a ½ to 2 inch (1.3 to 5 cm) width for larger images. A fine-tip brush is helpful when gluing small or delicate images, or when adding glue under the edges of paper. Decoupage medium washes out of most brushes with warm water as long as you're timely in your cleanup. After cleaning your brush, expel all of the excess water before dipping it back into the decoupage medium. Shake the brush firmly over the sink, or wrap it in a towel and squeeze the moisture out. Although you'll probably want to refrain from decoupaging with your best brushes, bear in mind that low-quality brushes are prone to loose bristles. These can get stuck in the glue and be hard to remove. Sponge brushes are a pleasant alternative. They evenly distribute decoupage medium, have no bristles, and cost very little. However, always monitor the amount of glue on your sponge

brush and err on the side of caution. Sponge brushes can quickly absorb too much decoupage medium and this will present problems. Fragile papers tend to tear when mounted with excessive glue. Never fully load your sponge brush with decoupage medium unless you need to cover a large area of glass in a short amount of time.

ADHESIVE

Decoupage medium is a specially formulated glue designed expressly as a paper adhesive. It can be found in any craft store and is offered in a range of finishes, such as matte, satin, semi-gloss, gloss, and high gloss. Decoupage medium is cloudy when applied but dries totally clear.

GLASS

Any smooth glass surface is a prime candidate for decoupage. Flat glass is the easiest foundation to work on, because you won't be challenged by curves. The demands of working on curved glass, however, are minor, and require only a little extra care.

PAPER

Images for decoupage can come from infinite sources. Magazines, catalogs, wrapping paper, and postcards all have interesting printed designs. A photocopier is a handy machine, because it can reduce or enlarge your selected image to fit your glass. It also generates multiples, allowing you to make a favorite image into a repeated motif. Making color photocopies of your photographs is a great way to incorporate treasured images into decoupaged glass. If you have a computer and printer, use them to create original graphic images, text, dingbats, or clip art. These look great in color or black and white. Scanning and manipulating

Assorted decoupage papers

photos or printed papers also can be fun. As you collect images over time, organize them by subject matter for future projects.

MAGNETS

Craft supply stores sell magnets in several forms. Some types are self-adhesive; they're manufactured on a backing paper that, once removed, exposes a sticky surface. Some magnets you'll have to glue to the glass yourself. This can be accomplished with a multi-use, high-strength epoxy (photo 6). Magnets sold in sheet and strip form can be cut to any size or shape. Other magnets, particularly the thicker and stronger ones, are sold in precut shapes.

Photo 6

THE PROCESS

The simple procedure for decoupaging glass is fairly consistent from project to project.

1. Select and carefully cut out your images. Determine their placement on the glass. You'll frequently be working on the back side of the glass with the image facing away from you. To know where to put the glue, you'll have to know where and in what direction the paper will be applied. If you plan to reverse decoupage many images into an overlapping composition, you'll need to know the order in which to apply them. This planning is important because decoupage medium dries quickly, and you'll need to work with as much speed as possible.

2. Remove any price stickers or labels from the glass, making sure to eliminate any residual adhesive. Use a paper towel or lint-free cloth to clean the surface of the glass with glass cleaner.

3. Paint a thin, even coat of decoupage medium onto the glass. The size of the area covered with glue should be at least as large as the paper being adhered. Decoupage medium can be applied to the paper first, but this is a risky approach. Paper that has been moistened with glue is more prone to tearing. The less the paper is handled in this fragile state, the better the results.

4. Position the paper over the decoupage medium and gently lay it down. You'll want to make sure no air bubbles are trapped between the image and the glass surface. Also, do your best to iron out any wrinkles in the paper and eliminate any excess decoupage medium. For small areas it's best to use your fingers to gently press and smooth the paper

Photo 7

Photo 8

(photo 7). Your fingertips are sensitive to any surface abnormalities. Begin in the center of the paper and work outward to the edges. A clean, lint-free cloth can be used instead of your fingers to flatten the glued paper. For larger areas, you may want to use a rubber roller, but proceed with caution across the paper to avoid rips.

5. Clean off any extra glue from around the edges of the paper before it dries. If an edge isn't sticking down, it may be due to a lack of adhesive. Using a

fine-tip paintbrush, carefully apply more decoupage medium under the loose edge.

6. If you're working in reverse on the back side of the glass, paint a thin layer of decoupage medium over the back side of the glued image to seal the paper in place (photo 8). If you're working on the front side of the glass, the paper will be sealed by the varnish in the next step. Allow all decoupage medium to dry thoroughly.

7. Decoupage medium can act as its own varnish. If you don't use the medium as a topcoat however, other options are available. Read the label of any varnish to make sure it's appropriate for both glass and paper. Incompatible varnishes can yellow paper over time and damage printed colors. A clear aerosol spray is a good varnish for glass decoupage. Use sprays in accordance with printed safety precautions in a well-ventilated and dust-free area. Spray the varnish using a horizontal motion beginning off one edge of the top of the project. Proceed with a continuous and light coat of spray across the project and off the opposite edge. Slightly overlap the layers of the varnish as you work your way down the project. Any area of glass that's missed in the initial spray will be covered in subsequent coatings. Be respectful of the varnish's drying time and try not to be in a hurry.

Assembly With Glass

A few projects in this section rely on the availability of custom-cut glass. This is an excellent opportunity to locate and support the glass professionals in your

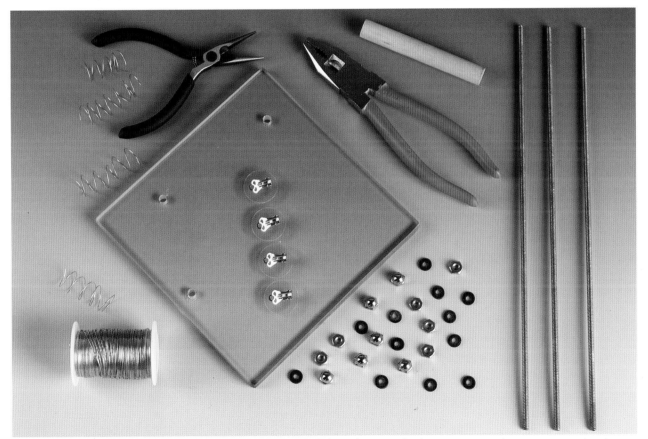

Left to right: decorative copper wire, needle-nose pliers, cut and drilled glass, clip earring backs, acorn nuts, washers, wire cutters, dowel, threaded rods

community. Their expertise can provide a wealth of information about the types and characteristics of commercial flat glass. Most glass businesses have a wide range of products, because they're regularly called on to service many needs. Professional glass cutters, or glaziers (a middle English term), can recommend the best type and thickness of glass for your project, cut it to size, and drill holes if needed. Artisans themselves, glaziers are often curious to see the creative ways in which flat glass is put to use.

Joining pieces of flat glass is an exciting area to explore. Look closely at the legs of Stands That Deliver on page 150 to see that they're actually cabinet handles. The Compact Disk Library on page 148 uses rigid cable, nuts, and bolts for support. Both projects rely on ordinary hardware to become contemporary works of art. The Woven Metal Coasters on page 145 are held together at the seams by copper foil tape, typically a stained glass supply. As you can see from these examples, there are many opportunities to craft ordinary flat glass into modern and elegant works of art.

GLASS BEADS

The amazing beauty and diversity of glass beads inspire countless craft ideas and innovations. Retail bead stores stock an overwhelming supply to dazzle and delight you. A basic supply of beads can be found at most craft supply stores, or surf the Internet and purchase beads online. With so many to choose from, selecting the beads to use for a project may be the most difficult step. Once your choices are made, projects such as the Goblet Keeper on page 152 are assembled with speed and ease by stringing beads on head pins (photo 9), then earring hoops (photo 10).

Photo 9

Photo 10

Bottle Cutting

Not only is bottle cutting a fun hobby, it's also an earth-friendly craft. Reclaiming used glassware and turning it into art reduces consumer waste, benefitting both your home and the environment. The simplest way to cut bottles is with a tool designed specifically for the job. Bottle cutters are sold in well-stocked craft supply stores. They're also available from stained glass suppliers and Internet retailers. Once you have a bottle cutter, ideas for projects spring up everywhere.

It takes practice to become a skillful bottle cutter. Your first attempts may vary in their success, but remember that it's part of the learning process. The most important step when starting out is to read your user's manual thoroughly. Carefully follow its guidelines for personal safety and operating instructions.

The basic steps in bottle cutting are scoring a line, tapping the glass, separating the pieces, and smoothing the edges. Once this is done, cut bottles are ready for further embellishment with many of the techniques described in this book: painting, etching, embellishment, and decoupage.

BOTTLES

There is a dazzling assortment of bottles to cut. Their sizes, colors, and shapes vary greatly. Hunting for interesting bottles is part of the fun of this craft. With tactful notification, your friends, family, and even local restauranteurs can be on the lookout for attractive specimens. Old bottles are still a bargain at garage sales and flea markets. They may need a little cleaning, but they have tons of character and design potential. See page 12 for glass cleaning tips. Glass bottles are manufactured under different circumstances in different facilities, and so they vary in thickness and uniformity. This causes each bottle to be unique in the way it responds to the cutter, heightening the value of repeated practice.

CLEANING

Completely remove both the paper label and its sticky adhesive before cutting a bottle. Labels interfere with the quality of the cut and, if left on the glass, adhesives cause your cutter blade to skip on the surface. If you attempt to remove labels from cut bottles, you put yourself at an unnecessary risk due

A variety of bottles, bottle cutter, safety goggles

to the sharp edges of the separated glass. If you have difficulty removing jar and bottle labels, try using one of the great products on the market that simplify this job.

SAFETY GOGGLES AND GLOVES

Whenever you use a bottle cutter, or grind and polish glass, it's important to protect your eyes with safety goggles. Safety glasses and ordinary eyeglasses won't provide sufficient defense from glass shards and dust. When cut into two, bottle edges are extremely sharp and should be handled with care. Leather work gloves afford the strongest protection for your hands. If you feel hampered by stiff leather gloves and their lack of mobility, canvas-backed rubber gardening gloves are an adequate substitute.

WORK SURFACE

Cover your work space with plenty of newspaper before beginning a bottle-cutting project. A wide stretch of newspaper provides a well-protected landing surface for glass shards or dust that travels far away from the cutter.

CUTTER OIL

Always keep the cutting wheel on your bottle cutter lubricated. Any brand of household lubricant or sewing-machine oil will do the job, and a single drop is sufficient. Relubricate the wheel before each cut. An unlubricated cutting wheel can damage your bottle and ruin the cutter's blade, so practice regular oiling.

MASKING TAPE

A piece of masking tape wrapped around the glass, underneath the score line, helps keep the score from traveling improperly when the bottle is tapped.

THE PROCESS

Getting Started

Although the temptation to immediately cut attractive bottles may be strong, it's advisable to begin this craft using inexpensive and plentiful recycled materials. Cutting beer bottles is a great way to become familiar with the performance of your new tool. Beer bottles are generally made from a thin glass that cuts with ease. Square or odd-shaped jars are more challenging to cut. It takes time before your results become consistent and predictable. Practice is the key to developing your skills. Save your best bottles until you're confident and experienced operating a bottle cutter.

Scoring

The cutting wheel scratches an even line around your bottle when it's positioned on the cutter and turned by hand. This light line is called a *score*, and creating it is the most critical step in bottle cutting. Accurate score lines lead to well-separated bottles. To make a score, position one hand on the bottle above the height you'll be cutting and one hand on the bottle below (photo 11). Apply gentle but contin-

Photo 11

uous pressure on the bottle, while simultaneously turning it against the wheel for one complete rotation. As you turn the bottle (always in the same direction), a light tearing sound can be heard. The bottle needs to be fully and evenly scored to insure a clean break. If your line is incomplete, re-score uncut areas only. Never cut twice over the same line.

The cutting wheel arm adjusts up and down to produce scores at different heights. The blade should always contact the glass at a 90° angle. The position of the cutting wheel will have to be changed to cut a bottle in a curve that doesn't fit this angle. Consult your bottle cutter's operating guide for instructions. If you've advanced to square or unusual-shaped bottles remember that the glass may be thicker in certain locations. While turning, you may need to exert extra pressure at these points.

Separating

Once your bottle is successfully scored, it's time to break the glass. Adhere a band of masking tape underneath the score line to inhibit it from moving beyond the intended breaking path. Insert the tapping arm into the neck of the bottle and lower it until its curved end is level with your score line. Pick a starting place and tap softly on the inside of the scored line. A slight crack or fracture will appear in the glass at the tapped point. When this occurs, move your tapping arm slightly ahead of the visible break and repeat the tapping process. After working your way around the bottle in this fashion, the bottle should easily separate. If it doesn't, re-tap any unfractured lines. If your breaking line travels away from the score, stop what you're doing and re-score a new line below the level of any fractures in the bottle.

Finishing

Cut bottles have sharp edges that require polishing. Luckily, there's an inexpensive and efficient way to achieve a smooth, finished appearance. You'll need a shallow metal baking pan (approximately 9 x 13 x 2 inches [22.9 x 33 x 5 cm] or larger), sanding paper in various grits, and water. Half fill the pan with water. Take the sandpaper with the coarsest grit, and submerse it into the pan with the abrasive side facing up. Place your bottle, cut side down, on top of the sandpaper. Rotate the cut bottle in a slow and gentle circular motion until the sharpest edges are worn away. Exchange the coarse sandpaper for a medium-grit sheet and repeat the process. For the finishing touch, make a third and final pass with the glass on a fine-grit, polishing-grade sandpaper. If your bottle needs sanding in hard-to-reach areas, work with a piece of wet sandpaper in a gloved hand or attach a small piece of wet sandpaper to a small dowel.

Polka-Dot Vase

Designer
TERRY
TAYLOR

THIS CHARMING POLKA-DOT VASE IS A MODEL OF UNDERSTATEMENT. ITS CAUTIOUS WHIMSY ENERGIZES ANY FLORAL ARRANGEMENT WITHOUT DUELING FOR ATTENTION. PUT BASIC ETCHING AND EMBELLISHMENT SKILLS TO WORK TO CREATE THIS DELIGHTFUL NEW VASE IN A SINGLE AFTERNOON.

What You Do

1 Clean all surfaces of the glass vase with glass cleaner and a paper towel or lint-free cloth.

2 On the heavyweight paper, measure and mark a 1-inch (2.5 cm) square. With scissors, cut out this square template. Place the self-adhesive vinyl on your work surface with the backing paper facing up. Trace around the template with the pencil 20 times to make 20 individual squares. Cut these squares out of the self-adhesive vinyl with scissors, and set them aside.

3 Select a coin or other round object to use as a second template. Center the coin on one square of the self-adhesive vinyl. The vinyl side of the square should be facing up. Trace around the coin with a pencil. Repeat this process until you've traced a circle in the center of all 20 vinyl squares.

4 Peel away the backing paper from one vinyl square and adhere the vinyl to the glass vase. Use the wooden or plastic spoon to secure the edges of the vinyl to the surface of the glass. Attach four other vinyl squares to the same side of the glass vase. Using the craft knife with the swivel blade, cut out the circles from the attached vinyl. Remove the cutout circles with the pick-out tool or the tip of a fixed-blade craft knife. Five vinyl stencils are now on the vase.

5 Spread the newspaper to cover and protect your work surface. Position the vase on top with the applied vinyl squares facing up. Prepare the etching cream. Pour a small amount of the cream onto one vinyl-covered square. Spread the cream with the squeegee evenly over the exposed glass circle. Repeat this process for the remaining vinyl stencils. Allow the cream to etch the surface of the glass. When the time has elapsed, rinse off the cream and dry the vase.

What You Need

Flat-sided glass vase

Glass half-marbles

Etching cream

Self-adhesive vinyl in white

Glass cleaner

Paper towels, or a lint-free cloth

Coins or another circular template

Craft knife with fixed and swivel blades

Glass epoxy

Squeegee

Pencil

Scissors

Wooden or plastic spoon

Heavyweight paper

Straightedge

Ruler

Newspaper

Pick-out tool, optional

6 Repeat steps 4 and 5 for the remaining sides of the vase, completing one side at a time.

7 Lay the etched vase on its side. Prepare to use the epoxy according to the manufacturer's directions. Glue one glass half-marble on or near each etched circle on one side of the vase. You can use strips of masking tape to hold the half-marbles in place until the epoxy dries. Allow the glue to completely dry before rotating the vase.

8 Repeat step 7 for each side of the vase.

Smashing Glass Baubles

Designer
TERRY TAYLOR

YOU'LL LOOK SENSATIONAL IN THIS FROSTED GLASS EARRING AND BROOCH ENSEMBLE. HUNTING FOR COLORED GLASS, SHATTERING IT INTO PIECES, AND TUMBLING IT TO A MATTE FINISH MEANS THIS JEWELRY IS JUST AS FUN TO MAKE AS IT IS TO WEAR. NO TWO PIECES WILL EVER LOOK THE SAME, SO YOU'RE GUARANTEED A UNIQUE ACCESSORY FOR ANY OCCASION.

What You Do

1 Create your own shards from attractive glass bottles or jars following the instructions on page 116.

2 Follow the manufacturer's instructions for operating the rock tumbler. Use the coarsest grit possible in the rock tumbler to achieve a frosted, matte finish on the shards and half-marbles. Tumble the glass for approximately six to eight hours. When the time has elapsed, check the progress of the finish on the glass. Continue to tumble the glass until you achieve the desired results.

3 Read and follow the instructions printed on the epoxy label. Glue the flat, back side of one tumbled glass half-marble to the front surface of a tumbled glass shard. Allow the adhesive to dry. Repeat this process to make as many pieces of jewelry as you desire.

4 Hold a purchased earring or brooch back behind one set of glued glass. If needed, trim the plastic on the jewelry back so it will hide behind the assembled glass. A fine-tooth jewelers' saw or a motorized cutting tool easily trims plastic jewelry backs.

5 Use the epoxy to glue one back onto each tumbled glass earring or brooch. Make sure the direction of the clip or pin is correct. Let the glue dry before trying on the jewelry.

What You Need

*Glass shards, similar in size and shape

*Glass half-marbles

Rock tumbler

Coarse grinding material

Glass epoxy

Earring backs, clip style

Brooch backs

Hammer

Towel

Safety goggles

Sturdy work gloves

Tile nippers, optional

Fine-tooth jewelers' saw, or motorized cutting tool, optional

*Pretumbled glass or real ocean glass also works well. If you use these items, skip steps 1 and 2.

Baroque in Glass Mirror

Designer TERRY TAYLOR

A CONTEMPORARY
WORK OF ART THAT'S
CHEERFUL, USEFUL,
AND SIMPLE TO
MAKE—SOUND TOO
GOOD TO BE TRUE?
ETCH, TUMBLE, AND
GLUE IS ALL YOU'VE
GOT TO DO TO ADD
THIS FRESH
COSMOPOLITAN
MIRROR TO
YOUR HOME.

What You Do

1 Clean the mirror with the glass cleaner and a paper towel or lint-free cloth.

2 Peel a corner of the backing paper away from the self-adhesive vinyl, and press the exposed adhesive to the mirror's edge. Slowly work your way across the entire surface of the mirror,

peeling away more backing paper and pressing down more vinyl as you go. Smooth out any air bubbles or wrinkles with the squeegee.

3 Measure and mark a line on the vinyl that is approximately ¾ inch (1.9 cm) inside the edge of the mirror. With the craft knife, trim the vinyl following this line. Remove the scored strip of self-adhesive vinyl from the edge of the mirror, leaving the center portion of the mirror covered. Use a wooden or plastic spoon to fasten the edges of the vinyl to the mirror. Remove any excess adhesive with a moist cotton-tipped swab.

4 Spread the newspaper to cover and protect your work surface, and position the mirror on top. Prepare the etching cream. Pour a small amount of the etching cream onto the vinyl-covered surface of the glass. With the squeegee, spread the cream evenly over the exposed edges of the mirror. Continue to pour and squeegee the cream onto the vinyl until the edge of the mirror is completely covered. Allow the cream to etch the surface of the mirror, then rinse the cream off the mirror with a damp sponge. The etched band around the mirror serves two purposes: its slightly rough surface bonds better with the glass epoxy, and it won't reflect the glass embellishments or the glass epoxy attached to the mirror.

5 Arrange the tumbled glass shards along the edge of the mirror, allowing some shards to slightly hang over. Glue the shards to the mirror one at a time following the procedure and safety precautions printed on the glass epoxy label. Allow the epoxy to dry.

6 Arrange one tumbled glass half-marble on top of each fixed glass shard. Glue the half-marbles to the shards one at a time, and let dry.

What You Need

Flat mirror

Etching cream

*Tumbled glass shards

*Tumbled glass half-marbles

Self-adhesive vinyl in white

Squeegee

Glass epoxy

Glass cleaner

Paper towels, or a lint-free cloth

Craft knife

Ruler

Pencil

Wooden or plastic spoon

Newspaper

Sponge

Water

Cotton-tipped swabs

*Tumbled glass (also called ocean or beach glass) is sold at most craft stores. If you're lucky enough to have a collection of genuine ocean glass gathered from the beach, you can use that as well. With a basic rock tumbler, you can create your own frosted glass in the colors you desire. Break glass bottles or jars according to the directions on page 116. Refer to page 117 for tumbling directions.

Sake Bottles Supreme

Designer
MARTHE LE VAN

WITH A NOD TO EASTERN
CULTURE, THESE FORMAL
BOTTLES BRING A TOUCH
OF CEREMONIAL DIGNITY TO
YOUR TABLE. DECOUPAGE
ANY CLEAR GLASS BOTTLE
WITH A STRIKING COLLAGE
OF HANDMADE PAPERS AND
METALLIC FOILS TO CREATE A
ONE-OF-A-KIND STATEMENT.
FILLED WITH SEASONED OILS
AND VINEGARS, THEY MAKE
GREAT LAST-MINUTE GIFTS.

What You Do

1 Use a measuring tape or piece of string to determine the circumference of the bottle at the points where you'll attach red handmade paper bands. This measurement tells you how long to cut the paper strips. Determine the width of the strips of red paper to complement the shape of the bottles.

2 Place the cutting board on your work surface, and lay the red paper on top. Position the straightedge or ruler on top of the handmade paper below its edge and equal to the width you intend to cut. Once square, hold the straightedge or ruler firmly in place as a guide, and cut the strip with the craft knife.

3 Repeat step 2 to make additional paper bands for the bottles. Vary the number and the thicknesses of the strips, as well as the paper used. You may want to cut additional strips to decoupage vertically, such as on the bottled pictured on the right.

4 Locate circular or oval objects to use as templates for cutting out other decorative elements. Place the object on top of the back side of a piece of decoupage paper. Trace the object onto the paper with a pencil. Cut out the traced circle or oval with scissors. These shapes provide background color and texture for the bottles.

5 The bold black icons on the front of the bottles are computer-generated. If you're unable to locate the specific font from which these icons were selected, photocopy the design template on page 134, sizing it to fit the bottle. Cut out the image.

6 Clean the bottle with glass cleaner and a paper towel or lint-free cloth.

What You Need

Clear glass bottles

Cork bottle tops

Handmade papers in red and ivory

Wrapping paper in metallic gold

Computer-generated dingbat, or photocopied design template (page 134)

Decoupage medium, matte finish

Flat paintbrush, 1 inch (2.5 cm) wide

Fine-tip artist's paintbrush

Stamping ink sponge dauber in metallic gold

Clear aerosol varnish

Glass cleaner

Paper towels, or a lint-free cloth

Measuring tape, or string

Scissors

Fixed-blade craft knife

Straightedge or ruler

Embroidery floss in red

Brass bead

Permanent marker in black

Cutting board

Pencil

Newspaper

7 Start with the strips of paper that encircle the bottles. Apply a small amount of the matte decoupage medium to the flat paintbrush. Spread the glue evenly on the front of the bottle for approximately one-quarter of the length of the strip. Lay the center of the paper strip on the bottle in the center of the glue with the front side of the paper facing up. With your fingers, lightly press the paper to the surface of the glass and smooth out any air bubbles or wrinkles. Rotate the bottle one-quarter turn. Add more glue next to the adhered section of paper, and press more of the strip of paper to the glass. Continue around the bottle until the band is completely in place, keeping the band level as you work.

8 Clean off any excess decoupage medium that seeped out from under the edges of the paper. Allow the decoupage medium to dry. You can look through the bottle to the back side of the facing paper to monitor the drying progress.

9 Repeat steps 7 and 8 for each band of paper.

10 Decoupage the remaining decorative elements such as the circles of colored paper and the icons. Wait until the glue behind one element is completely dry before applying an overlapping element.

11 On the square bottle, metallic gold stamping ink was sponge-daubed onto the thick bands of red paper. Add any additional embellishments to the decoupaged bottle at this time.

12 Stand the bottles up on newspaper, and seal them with the spray varnish following the directions on page 139 step 8.

13 To decorate the neck of the bottle with embroidery floss, use the fine-tip artist's paintbrush and matte-finish decoupage medium. Begin on the back side of the bottle and apply a small amount of glue just underneath the bottle's lip. Press one end of the embroidery floss into the glue. Continue around the upper part of the neck, painting on glue and pressing down floss in small increments. Work in circles around and down the neck, keeping the layers of floss as close together as possible. When the neck is sufficiently covered, end the application of floss on the back of the bottle. Trim the end of the floss, coat it with glue, and tuck it into the preceding row.

14 Repeat step 13 to decorate the cork. Before you begin, place the cork firmly in the bottle. Mark the cork above the mouth of the bottle so you'll know where to stop attaching the floss. Color the tops of the corks and the floss-free area of cork inside the mouth of the bottle with a black permanent marker.

15 String the brass bead on a small length of embroidery floss to make a necklace for the bottle, as shown on the left.

Magnetic Personality

Designer
MARTHE LE VAN

FINALLY, REFRIGERATOR MAGNETS
THAT ARE JUST AS PRECIOUS AS
THE PRIZED DRAWINGS AND
PHOTOGRAPHS THEY
HOLD. BECAUSE
THEY'RE MADE FROM
CLEAR GLASS AND DECOUPAGE
PAPER, YOU CAN CREATE A SET
OF MAGNETS TO FIT A THEME,
MATCH A ROOM, OR SPELL A
NAME. GO AHEAD—
EXPRESS YOURSELF.

What You Do

1 Cut the selected images out of the decoupage paper with scissors, allowing a generous border on all sides. A square of decoupage paper that's 2 x 2 inches (5 x 5 cm) accommodates both large and small half-marbles. Make sure the picture or pattern you want to show through the half-marble is in the center of the square.

2 The quality of the half-marbles varies greatly, even within the same package. Look closely at the half-marbles and discard those that are cracked, scratched, or have large bubbles in the glass. Clean the flat surface of one half-marble with glass cleaner and a paper towel or lint-free cloth.

3 Dip the 1-inch (2.5 cm) paintbrush into the matte decoupage medium and apply a thin, even coat to the flat surface of the half-marble. Place the marble on the center of one paper square. Lift the marble and paper off your work surface and squeeze them together. This distributes the decoupage medium and allows you to see the position of the image. While the glue is still wet, small adjustments can be made in the paper's placement, but be careful not to cause wrinkles or tears. Let the glue dry completely. Repeat this process for all the marbles, letting them dry before proceeding to step 4.

4 Use scissors to trim away the excess paper from the marble. Because they have a curved surface, it's easy to make a close cut that's slightly underneath the outer edge of the glass. With the fine-tip artist's paintbrush, re-glue any paper edges as needed. Allow this glue to dry.

What You Need

Clear glass half-marbles

Decoupage papers

Decoupage medium, matte and gloss finish

Flat paintbrush, 1 inch (2.5 cm) wide

Fine-tip artist's paintbrush

Glass cleaner

Paper towels, or a lint-free cloth

Scissors

Fixed-blade craft knife

5 Paint a thin topcoat of gloss-finish decoupage medium over the back of the paper with a 1-inch (2.5 cm) sponge brush. Let the glue dry. The glue acts as a varnish and gives the back of the magnets a nice finish.

6 Precut, round magnets ¼ inch (6 mm) thick were used for their incredible strength. Individual magnets were glued to the paper-backed glass with a few drops of epoxy. The decoupaged half-marbles and magnets were held together firmly until the epoxy formed a tight bond. For other magnet options, see page 119.

Spring Dream Dishes

Designer
MARTHE LE VAN

BUTTERFLIES FROLIC AMONG LUSH BLOSSOMS ON THESE GARDEN PARTY PLATES. LIGHT PASSES SOFTLY

THROUGH A PASTEL PALETTE OF TRANSLUCENT PAPERS DECOUPAGED IN REVERSE. DISPLAYED ON A STAND

OR FILLED WITH POTPOURRI PETALS, THESE PLATES SPREAD CHEER WHEREVER THEY ALIGHT.

What You Do

1   Determine which images will make an appealing collage and carefully cut them out of the napkins. Position the cutouts on the plates as you go along. This helps to refine the final layout and to monitor how many cutout images are ultimately needed.

2   Place the light-colored scrap paper on your work surface. You'll need a neutral background over which to consider image placement. Clean the back surface of the plate with glass cleaner and a paper towel or lint-free cloth. Place the plate on the scrap paper with the back side facing up.

3   The paper napkins may be up to three layers thick. To achieve the most transparency, peel away the bottom two layers and work only with the upper printed surface. The single-ply napkin is a much more delicate paper to decoupage, but it will provide a more luminous result. Single-ply images also bring an additional depth to your composition when overlapped. Peel the backing layers away just before gluing down the image. Select an area on the back of the plate to start the decoupage. Remember that you're working in reverse, so the images at the forefront of the design need to be applied first.

4   Apply a small amount of the decoupage medium to the 1-inch-wide (2.5 cm) paintbrush. Spread the glue evenly on the glass. The surface area covered by the glue should be slightly larger than the surface area of the image you're decoupaging. Lay the paper onto the plate in the center of the glue with the image side facing the glue. With your fingers, lightly press the paper to

What You Need

1 clear, round glass dinner plate

1 clear, round glass dessert plate

Floral-printed paper napkins

Tissue paper, full sheets in white and pink

Decoupage medium, matte finish

Flat paintbrush, 1 inch (2.5 cm) wide

Flat paintbrush, 2 inches (5 cm) wide

Fine-tip artist's paintbrush

Clear aerosol varnish

Glass cleaner

Paper towels, or a lint-free cloth

Scissors

Fixed-blade craft knife

Light-colored scrap paper

Cutting board

Newspaper

the surface of the glass to form a secure bond, and smooth out all air bubbles and wrinkles in the paper. Once you've decoupaged an image to your liking, seal it in place by applying a thin coat of glue across the back side of the image and slightly off all the edges of the paper. Allow the decoupage medium to dry.

5 Repeat step 4 for all remaining images. Allow the glue to dry between each paper application. If you're having trouble working in reverse, lift the plate up by its edge and turn it towards you to reconfirm image placement.

6 Once the collage is complete, you'll decoupage one large piece of tissue paper for the background color. Dip the 2-inch-wide (5 cm) paintbrush into the decoupage medium. Work quickly to apply a thin, even coating of the glue over the entire decoupaged surface of the plate. Center the piece of tissue paper over the plate and gently lay it down on top of the decoupage medium. Press the tissue to the glass in the middle of the plate. Use your fingers to smooth the tissue gradually across the surface of the plate. Flatten wrinkles and air pockets as you work your way to the edges. Because the plate has a curved surface, some minor wrinkling will occur. Fortunately, decoupaged tissue paper is so light in weight and color that the wrinkles are barely visible once the glue dries. If you find the background color to be too light, add a second layer of tissue paper by repeating this step. Allow the decoupage medium to dry longer than usual, ideally overnight.

7 Use scissors to trim the excess tissue paper to a 1-inch (2.5 cm) border around the plate. With the plate upside down on the cutting board, follow around the edge of the glass with a fixed-blade craft knife and cut away all surplus tissue. Glue down any loose edges with a little decoupage medium and the fine-tip artist's brush.

8 When using spray varnish, it's best to work in a well-ventilated, dust-free area. Lay the decoupaged plate face down on a surface covered with newspaper. Spray the varnish using a horizontal motion beginning off one edge of the top of the project. Proceed with a continuous, light coat of spray across the project and off the opposite edge. Slightly overlap the layers of the varnish as you work your way down the plate. Any area of the plate missed in the initial spray will be covered in subsequent coatings. Be respectful of the varnish's drying time and try not to get in a hurry. Two to three coats of varnish will adequately seal the plate.

Quaint Cut-Bottle Vases

Designer

MARGARET SPRAGUE

SOME GLASS BOTTLES AND JARS ARE WONDERFUL ON THEIR OWN. AFTER A GOOD CUT, THE BEST EXAMPLES MAY REQUIRE NO FURTHER EMBELLISHMENT. WITH THE ADDITION OF A FROG OR OASIS, THESE TEAL CUBES MAKE EXCELLENT CONTAINERS FOR LOW FLORAL ARRANGEMENTS. ONCE YOU'VE GAINED EXPERIENCE CUTTING ROUND GLASSES, MOVE ON TO THE CHALLENGE OF THICKER, MORE ODDLY SHAPED BOTTLES.

What You Do

1 Remove any labels and adhesive residue from the glass. Clean the glass thoroughly with warm, soapy water. Refer to page 12 for tips on cleaning old bottles. Towel dry the glass.

2 Spread a generous amount of newspaper across your work surface. Put on the safety goggles and heavy work gloves. Adjust the height of the cutting wheel arm to the desired location on the bottle. The vases can be the same height, as shown, or different heights. Lubricate the cutting wheel with household or sewing-machine oil before each cut. Following the manufacturer's instructions, use the bottle cutter to score the bottles or jars one at a time. Be sure to leave a wide enough opening in the glass to insert a floral frog or oasis.

3 Adhere a layer of masking tape around each bottle or jar directly below the score line to promote the accuracy of the break. Working from the inside, use the bottle cutter's tapping arm to fracture each score line. Separate the bottles or jars.

4 Fill a metal baking pan halfway with water and submerse a sheet of coarse-grit sandpaper with the abrasive side facing up. One at a time, smooth the cut edges of the bottles or jars by rotating them in a slow circular motion over the coarse sandpaper. Repeat this process with a medium-grit and then a polishing-grade sandpaper.

5 Clean your new vases with glass cleaner and a paper towel or lint-free cloth. Place a floral frog or oasis in the base of each vase, and add water prior to creating a flower arrangement.

What You Need

2 square glass bottles or jars

Bottle cutter

Bottle cutter oil

Sandpapers in coarse, medium, and polishing grade grits

Baking pan

Safety goggles

Sturdy work gloves

Newspaper

Masking tape

Water

Floral frog or oasis

Cobalt Cut-Bottle Luminaria

Designer
TERRY TAYLOR

As night falls, let this
magnificent centerpiece
illuminate your tabletop
with a captivating glow.
Make this contemporary
project for your next
gathering with the help
of a bottle cutter and a
metal tomato cage.

What You Do

1 Remove all labels and adhesive residue from the bottles. Clean the glass with warm, soapy water and towel dry.

2 Spread a generous amount of newspaper across your work surface. Put on the safety goggles and heavy work gloves. Following the manufacturer's instructions, use the bottle cutter to score the bottles one at a time. Lubricate the cutting wheel with household or sewing-machine oil before each cut. Adjust the height of the cutting wheel to produce different sized candleholders. Be sure to leave a wide enough opening in the glass to insert a votive candle, tea light, or fuel cell.

3 Adhere a layer of masking tape around each bottle directly below the score line to promote the accuracy of the break. Working from the inside of the bottles, use the bottle cutter's tapping arm to fracture each score line. Separate the bottles.

4 Fill a metal baking pan halfway with water and submerge a sheet of coarse sandpaper with the abrasive side facing up. One at a time, smooth the cut edges of the bottles by rotating them in a slow circular motion over the coarse sandpaper. Repeat this process with a medium-grit, then a polishing-grade sandpaper.

5 With the wire cutters, trim two lengths of the 22-gauge wire for each bottle. Each length of wire should measure 36 inches (.9 m).

6 Cross two wire lengths to form an X shape. Twist the wires together at their center point. Turn one cut bottle upside down on your work surface. Place the crossed wires on the bottom of the bottle and temporarily secure them with a piece of masking tape.

What You Need

Glass bottles

Bottle cutter

Bottle cutter oil

22-gauge galvanized wire

Broomstick, or ¾-inch (2 cm) dowel, 12 inches (31 cm) long

Sandpapers in coarse, medium, and polishing-grade grits

Baking pan

Safety goggles

Sturdy work gloves

Wire cutters

Masking tape

Ruler

Needle-nose pliers

General-purpose pliers

Newspaper

Water

Towel

Wire tomato cage

Foliage

Votives, tea lights, or candle fuel cells

7 Turn the bottle right side up. Use your fingers to smooth and shape the four wires up the sides of the bottle. Secure the wires about halfway up the sides of the bottle with masking tape. These four wires become your hanger wires. Set the bottle aside and repeat steps 6 and 7 for the remaining cut bottles.

8 Make a long coil by wrapping the 22-gauge wire 20 or more times around the broomstick or dowel. Keep the spirals of the wire close together. Wind the wire many more times than you think you'll need to wrap around the top of each cut bottle.

9 Remove the coil from the broomstick or dowel. Splay out the loops of wire one by one, holding them firmly between your fingers and thumb.

Keep splaying out the loops until the entire coil is flattened. The loops will look slightly oval, but you can round each oval later with your fingers.

10 Wrap the full length of flattened coil around the top of one cut bottle. Use wire cutters to cut the exact length of coil needed to encircle the top of the bottle. Set aside the extra coil. Use your fingers and pliers (if needed) to wind the length of one of the hanger wires to a point on the flattened coil. Secure the coil around the bottle with the three remaining wires. Repeat this process for each cut bottle.

11 Gather the four hanger wires together on one cut bottle. Twist them loosely with your fingers about 4 inches (10.5 cm) above the rim of the bottle. Hold the loose twist in place with general-purpose pliers and use the needle-nosed pliers to tightly twist about 1 inch (2.5 cm) of the four wires together. Cut off the excess, untwisted wire with the wire cutters. Make a simple hook with the needle-nosed pliers at the end of the twisted wires. Repeat for all the bottles.

12 Turn the tomato cage upside down and place it on your work surface. Bend back each of the four legs into an attractive spiral design with the needle-nose pliers. Wrap vines of fresh ivy or other foliage around the frame of the tomato cage. Place votives, tea lights, or candle fuel cells in the cut bottles. Hang the cut bottle lights on the support wires of the tomato cage.

Woven Copper Coasters

8 pieces of flat glass, 4 x 4 inches (10.2 x 10.2 cm) each

8 strips of 36-gauge copper tooling foil, 12 x ½ inches (30.5 x 1.3 cm) each

3 yards (2.7 m) of ½-inch-wide (1.3 cm) copper foil tape with adhesive backing

Glass cleaner

Paper towels, or a lint-free cloth

Needle-nose pliers

Tin snips

Candle

Matches or lighter

Scissors

Burnishing tool

Designer
TRAVIS WALDRON

GORGEOUS ON BOTH SIDES, THESE STRIKING COASTERS ARE A TASTEFUL TOUCH ON ANY TABLE. USING JUST A FEW COMMON MATERIALS, YOU CAN ASSEMBLE THEM IN SHORT ORDER. WRAPPED IN A SMALL BOX THAT TRAVELS LIGHT, THEY CAN BE PACKED FOR YOUR NEXT WEEKEND GETAWAY AND PRESENTED WITH GRATITUDE TO YOUR HOST.

What You Do

1 Clean both sides of the glass pieces with the glass cleaner and a paper towel or lint-free cloth. Set them aside.

2 Light the candle. Holding one 12-inch (30.5 cm) copper strip with the needle-nose pliers grasping its middle, slowly pass the entire length of the strip over the candle flame to make attractive, lasting color changes in the copper. Any soot that forms underneath will be cleaned off later. Heat three more strips using the same technique.

3 Clean any soot off the strips with the glass cleaner and a paper towel or lint-free cloth. You now have four strips of intentionally tarnished copper and four strips of plain copper. With the tin snips, cut all the strips into pieces about 3 inches (7.6 cm) long (don't be too exact—when you weave the pieces, uneven edges will be desired).

4 Now you're ready to weave together four plain and four tarnished pieces of copper for each coaster. Place four pieces side by side, alternating the plain and tarnished pieces, and do a simple over-and-under weave of the four remaining pieces, also alternating plain and tarnished. Repeat until you've woven the copper for a total of four coasters.

5 Hold the edges with your fingertips, and place one piece of glass on your work surface. Make sure the glass is fingerprint- and dust-free. Place a woven piece in the center and sandwich it with a second piece of glass. Check again for position and any dust that needs removing.

6 Cut four 4⅛-inch (10.5 cm) pieces of copper foil tape. Peel ¼ inch (6 mm) of the backing paper away from one strip, exposing the adhesive. Set aside.

7 Carefully lift the sandwich, maintaining steady pressure on both pieces of glass to keep the woven copper from shifting. Adhere the exposed adhesive end of the copper foil tape to the corner of the sandwich, centering it over the two pieces of glass. Slowly peel away the rest of the backing paper while adhering the tape to the entire length of one side of the glass. Trim any excess tape with scissors. You'll note that the tape is wider than the edge of the sandwich. Fold down the extra tape on both sides of the sandwich, pressing firmly to adhere it to the glass and complete the seal.

8 Apply another piece of foil tape to the opposite side of the sandwich in the same manner, then repeat the process on the two remaining sides.

9 Construct and seal the three remaining coasters.

10 Use the burnishing tool to firmly and repeatedly rub the foil on all four sides and edges of each coaster to ensure a good bond, then clean the surface with glass cleaner.

Compact Disc Library

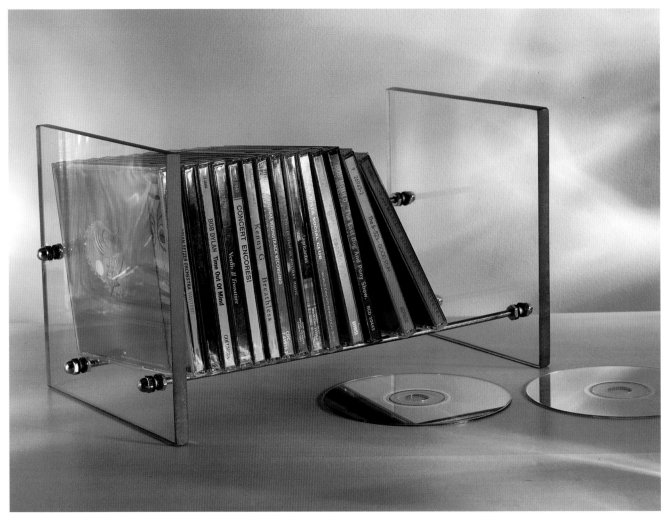

Designer
TERRY TAYLOR

PROCLAIM YOUR LOVE OF SIMPLICITY WITH THIS HANDSOME AND USEFUL COMPACT DISC SHELF. TWO PIECES OF TRANSPARENT GLASS ARE JOINED WITH INDUSTRIAL HARDWARE TO MAKE A BOLD DESIGN STATEMENT. THE PERFECT SIZE FOR YOUR HOME OR OFFICE DESKTOP, THIS STYLISH PIECE IS SO EASY TO PUT TOGETHER.

What You Do

1 Visit your local glass supplier, and take along the template and at least one piece of the threaded rod. The template shows the glazier the position for the holes to be drilled. The threaded rod provides a guide for the holes' diameter. Have the glazier cut, drill, and polish the edges of the two glass squares.

2 Place one nut at each end of one threaded rod. Screw the nuts onto the rod about 1 inch (2.5 cm) from each end. Slide one rubber washer on both ends of each rod. Push the washers along the rod towards the nuts. Repeat this process for the two remaining rods.

3 Place the rods into the holes of one glass square. On the outer surface of the glass shelf, slide a rubber washer onto the rod. Finger-tighten the acorn nuts onto the rods on the outer surface of the glass. Tighten the inner nuts flush against the glass.

4 Repeat step 3 with the second square of glass. Once your new shelf is fully assembled, clean the glass with glass cleaner and a paper towel or lint-free cloth.

5 Leave the clear glass unadorned to view the cover art on your favorite compact discs, or decorate the glass surfaces with paints, etching, or by adhering glass embellishments.

What You Need

2 custom-cut pieces of ⅜-inch-thick (9.5 mm) glass, each 6 ¾ inches (17.1 cm) square

Photocopy of design template (below) sized to fit your glass 3 threaded rods, size 10–24, each 12 inches (30.5 cm) long

6 acorn nuts, size 10–24

6 nuts, size 10–24

12 small rubber washers, the size of the regular nuts

It's possible to extend the length of the CD library. To accomplish this, you need to purchase longer threaded rods and have an additional square of glass cut to support the center weight. This additional piece of glass requires additional washers and nuts.

Stands That Deliver

Designer
TERRY TAYLOR

TREAT YOUR GARDEN-FRESH HARVEST OR NEWLY BLOOMING BULBS TO A MORE NOBLE STATION ATOP THESE

SLEEK STANDS. THE SMOKY GLASS AND METAL LEGS FLATTER WHATEVER YOU DISPLAY. DECIDING WHAT

HARDWARE TO USE FOR THE LEGS IS THE MOST DIFFICULT TASK IN THE PROJECT. MAKE YOUR HARDWARE

SELECTION FIRST, THEN TAKE THE LEGS AND THE TEMPLATE TO YOUR LOCAL GLASS SUPPLIER.

What You Do

1 Purchase the hardware to use as the legs of the stand. The designer chose two large drawer pulls for the larger stand and two smaller curved pulls for the smaller stand. You may prefer pulls in other materials such as brass, acrylic, or glass. Above all, make sure a machine screw fits into the pull's threaded receptacle. Some pulls use nuts and washers for installing the screws to the drawer, which won't work for this project.

2 Determine the size of the stand you'd like to make, and roughly sketch it onto the heavyweight paper. Try the pulls in several arrangements on top of the sketch to determine foot position. Keep in mind that most glass shops prefer to drill holes that are 1 inch (2.5 cm) from the edge of the glass. Once you're satisfied with the dimensions of the stand, draw a template for the glass using the ruler and the pen or pencil. Cut the template out of the paper with the scissors or craft knife. Reposition the hardware on the template and mark its location. Repeat step 2 for any additional stands.

3 Visit your local glass supplier with the template or templates in hand. Select the color of glass you'd like to use and the finish you'd like on the edges. It's a good idea to leave the hardware at the glass shop. While the glaziers are cutting the glass, they can reconfirm the hardware's fit with the holes they're drilling.

4 When the glass is cut and you've checked the hardware for an accurate fit, take the glass home. Attach the feet with the ⅝-inch (1.6 cm) machine screws. Slip rubber or fiber washers between the screw head, the glass, and the hardware before tightening the machine screw with the screwdriver.

What You Need

1 custom-cut piece of smoky glass per stand, ¼ inch (6 mm) thick

2 drawer or cabinet pulls per stand

⅝-inch (1.6 cm) machine screws, compatible with the pulls

Rubber or fiber washers, compatible with the machine screws

Heavyweight paper

Ruler

Pencil, or pen

Scissors, or craft knife

Screwdriver

Jewelry oxidizer, optional*

* This supply is available at most bead stores. The designer used it to darken the screw heads so they would blend in with the smoky glass.

5 Following the manufacturer's instructions, oxidize the finish on the screw heads to blend with the smoky glass (optional).

Goblet Keeper

Designer
MARTHE LE VAN

THESE BEADED GLASS "NAME TAGS" WRAP AROUND THE STEM OF A WINE GLASS FOR EASY IDENTIFICATION.

PARTY GUESTS CAN KEEP THE SAME CHARMED GLASS ALL NIGHT LONG, WHILE YOU KEEP

CLEANING AND CONFUSION TO A MINIMUM. SIMPLE AS STRINGING BEADS, THIS ENTERTAINING

PROJECT IS SURE TO GET YOU IN THE MOOD FOR A CELEBRATION.

What You Need

Earring hoops, large enough to fit around a goblet stem

Beading head pins

Antique glass beads

Glass seed beads

Round-nose pliers

Needle-nose pliers

Wire cutters

What You Do

1 Design the sequence of the beads, and estimate how many you'll need to fill an earring hoop.

2 The vertical beads or series of beads to be strung on the hoop are assembled on individual head pins. A head pin is made of flexible metal, and ranges from 2 to 3 inches (5 to 7.5 cm) in length. Purchase head pins that match the earring hoops and accommodate the beads you've selected. Both the width of the pin and the diameter of the head should be checked with the beads for a good fit. This is especially important when stringing antique beads.

3 String the beads on the head pin in hanging order from bottom to top. Use the round-nose pliers to create a hanging loop in the head pin wire as close to the top of the bead sequence as possible. Cut off the excess head pin above the hanging loop with the wire cutters.

4 Open the clasp of one earring hoop and straighten one end of the wire with the needle-nose pliers. Thread the beads and head pins onto the hoop in the order of your design. After the beads are strung on the hoop, use the needle-nose pliers to bend the hoop clasp back into its original angle.

5 You may find that your design has too many or too few beads for the hoop. If necessary, redesign the sequence by trading bead positions and adding or subtracting seed beads as filler.

6 Once the charm is complete, simply unfasten the hoop, place it around the stem of the wine goblet, and reattach the clasp. Splay the glass beads around the foot of the goblet for the best display.

FANCIFUL TRIFLE TUREEN, PAGE 22

STARLIGHT LANTERN, PAGE 58

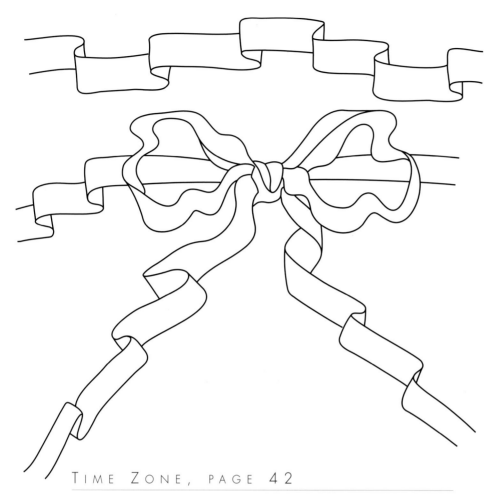

TIME ZONE, PAGE 42

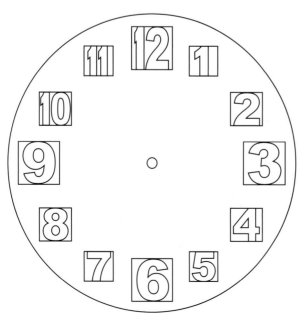

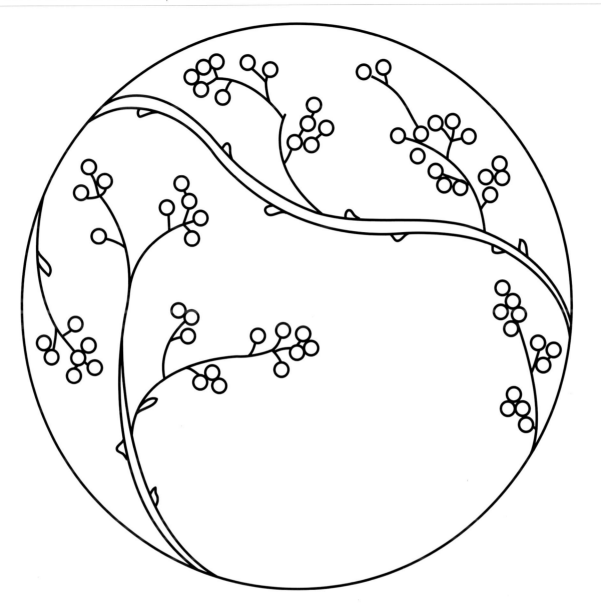

CHARMING SWARMING VASES, PAGE 18

Contributing Designers

MARTHE LE VAN

first encountered a decoupaged glass plate while rummaging at a local antiques shop. Inspired to make her own, she has been cheerfully decoupaging glassware ever since.

DIANA LIGHT

creates magic in glass by etching and painting fine art glass, mirrors, and functional pieces. Her designs and artwork are distributed worldwide from her studio in the mountains of North Carolina. You can contact Diana at dianalight@hotmail.com

JENNIFER E. MITCHELL

creates whimsical and inspiring mobiles with sheet glass, *dalles de verre*, and handblown glass in a variety of shapes and colors. She lives in beautiful, historic Portsmouth, New Hampshire, with her son, Aidan, husband, Robert, two dogs, and one cat. Besides making glass art, Jen enjoys roaming her gardens, visiting the nearby ocean, and exposing her son to the beauty of artistic expression. Visit Jen's website at www.stainedglassmobiles.com.

CHRISTINE KELLMANN STEVENSON

has had her owned stained glass business since 1988. Stevenson Stained Glass specializes in custom designed creations, instruction, tools, and supplies. Chris creates award-winning stained glass installations for new home construction in western North Carolina. With her husband, Ed, and her Old English Sheepdog, Baggins, by her side, she has found the mountains to be an inspiring place to practice her creative talents. A native of Wisconsin, Chris holds a BS in science from the University of Wisconsin-Milwaukee, and a Master of Arts and post graduate work in Education from the University of Mississippi. She is twice past-President of the Piedmont Handcrafters Association. Currently she is Secretary of the Sky-HY Chapter, American Business Women's Associationn, and member of the Asheville Area Chamber of Commerce, the Stained Glass Association of America, and Art Glass Suppliers Association.

TERRY TAYLOR

is an artist and designer. He has worked at Lark Books for several years wearing a variety of hats. His job du jour includes conceiving and executing projects for many Lark Books, in addition to writing and editing his own books.

TRAVIS WALDRON

is a semi-retired feminist psychotherapist who now runs her own fiber art and textile design studio, Wicked by Nature. She resides with her two dogs and visiting strays in the mountains outside Asheville, North Carolina.

Acknowledgments

S P E C I A L   T H A N K S   T O :

Cheryl Bly of Plaid Enterprises

Barb Bosler of B & B Etching Products

Susan Henshau of Armour Products

Kim Latham of Delta Technological Coatings

Angela Scherz of Pebeo

Peter Alberice, whose paintings appear on pages
24 and 150

The Natural Home in Asheville, North Carolina

Jay Musler's glasses (page 145) appear courtesy of
the Maurine Littleton Gallery

Barbara Zaretsky's postcards of Japanese art
appear on page 135.

Index